Great Brand Stories
Scotch Whisky

CREATIVE FIRE
THE STORY OF SCOTLAND'S
GREATEST EXPORT

Stuart Delves

CYANBOOKS

Copyright © 2007 Stuart Delves

First published in 2007 by Cyan Books, an imprint of

Cyan Communications Limited
119 Wardour Street
London W1F 0UW
United Kingdom
T: +44 (0)20 7565 6120
E: sales@cyanbooks.com
www.cyanbooks.com

A CIP record for this book is available from the British Library.

ISBN-13 978-1-904879-71-8
ISBN-10 1-904879-71-3

Book design: So... *www.soitbegins.co.uk*

Printed and bound in Great Britain by
TJ International Ltd, Padstow, Cornwall

For Catriona
Usually a flute of champagne
Or a glass of Chablis
But occasionally
When snow blankets the eaves
And icicles fringe the house
Like teeth:
A hot toddy.

"Whisky ... is masculine and penetrative. It can be coarse and aggressive. But perfectly conceived, it is creative fire."

Neil Gunn, *Whisky and Scotland*, 1935

"You could liken the range of aromas of Scotch Whisky to the range of octaves on a grand piano. The range of gin would be like that of a wood instrument; vodka a didgeridoo."

Rachel Barrie,
master blender for Glenmorangie, 2005

CONTENTS

PREFACE

Can I see the label? This is one of the everyday questions that has occupied people since the development of branding, as we have come to know it, in the nineteenth century. Back then, the label was still a relative innovation, used by manufacturers to give customers a reassurance about quality. By proclaiming ownership on a label, the manufacturer could try to guarantee the quality and consistency of the product – and build loyalty to that "brand".

Nowhere was this more evident than in the drinks industry, in particular whisky. With glass expensive, bottles with labels became prevalent only in late Victorian times. Until then, whisky was frequently sold in jugs, and the practice was open to abuse and adulteration. The bottle with a label gave the manufacturers greater quality control – and the medium to create brands.

Over the years, many different whisky brands came into being. Johnnie Walker is still walking, sometimes pursued by a White Horse or a Famous Grouse. Individual Scotch Whisky brands are very familiar to us, even if we are not all whisky drinkers. But it seems to me that there is something about Scotch Whisky itself – the idea, the story, the legend – that reaches deeper into our consciousness than any of the individual brands do.

I put this point to Stuart Delves when I first suggested this book to him. I have known Stuart for ten years. When I first met him he was a writer in a design company, and he was working on Scotch

Whisky brands among many other projects. Now he runs his own writing company, Henzteeth, which continues to work with Scotch Whisky brands. As I have got to know Stuart over the years, what I have come to admire, above all else, is his ability to write a story – to use detail, incident, character, place and often lyrical language to engage with readers. But, more than that, I value his intuitive understanding of the power of storytelling and its role in modern business.

This combination of whisky knowledge (not gained through over-indulgence) and a feeling for storytelling makes Stuart Delves the natural person to write this book. *Creative Fire* is a wonderful, dramatic and romantic gathering of stories that will increase your understanding of Scotch Whisky in every aspect. It deserves to be read in the flickering light of a log fire with a glass of an appropriate golden liquid in your hand. When seen through the lens of a brand, when compared and contrasted to conventional brands, Scotch Whisky develops extra layers of narrative depth. Stuart digs down through these sometimes peaty layers and tells stories that capture your imagination. And, in doing so, he allows you to discover that there is much more creativity, playfulness and intellect in the world of branding than you might ever have imagined.

John Simmons
Series editor, *Great brand stories*

INTRODUCTION

When John Simmons, series editor of *Great brand stories*, asked me if I'd like to submit a proposal for a book on Scotch Whisky, the brand, I was both delighted and slightly daunted. This would not be the story of Scotch Whisky the spirit – although of course that story would inform mine – or the story of the Scotch Whisky industry. This was to be the story of a meta-brand: the image and personality of a generic product. Fine. OK. But the thing is there's nothing generic about Scotch Whisky. Not only are there over 200 brands in the UK alone, there are different categories of whisky and endless different expressions within those categories. Scotch Whisky is a world: a world with worlds within. I was going to have to take some poetic licence.

Scotch is a phenomenon: it's exported to 200 countries around the world (France and Spain, the two biggest markets being jointly worth over £525m) and in 2001, for the first time, over one billion bottles were shipped overseas. Scotch is also unique – no other product, in any category, anywhere in the world, is named after its country of origin. Champagne and Cognac are the closest it gets elsewhere. But they're named after regions. Scotch is named after a country and under UK law a Scotch Whisky can only be described as made in Scotland if it has been matured in casks in a warehouse in Scotland for at least three years. And every brand of whisky that is distilled in Scotland bears the descriptor: Scotch Whisky. And proud of

DEWAR'S ADVERTISEMENT FROM 1906. THE N.B. AFTER PERTH STANDS FOR NORTH BRITAIN.

it. Further, even the spelling of Whisky when combined with Scotch is spelt differently from the grain spirits of Ireland and America, eschewing the superfluous "e". The identity of Scotch is intrinsically tied up with the identity of Scotland.

Scotch is a subject that people can and do get obsessed about. It can make fully grown men in suits and ties and sensible haircuts wax lyrical. It can make whisky critics write the most outlandish tasting notes (likening flavours to old leather car

LABEL DATING FROM 1936. NOTE IT WAS BOTTLED FOR A WINE MERCHANT – A COMMON PRACTICE AT ONE TIME.

seats or burnt creosote). It can make collectors out of the unsuspecting and send the staunchly constituted off on unhurried pilgrimages across the Highlands and Islands. Scotch Whisky has its enthusiasts, its devotees and its aficionados as well as its connoisseurs. Laphroaig, along with many another leading brand, has its advocates, and The Macallan even has a salaried ambassador based in New York (now there's a job to die for).

Books have been written about Scotch Whisky and there are magazines and websites devoted to the subject. But this book is different. Most tend to either look at the history of Scotch, provide an exhaustive A–Z of all the distilleries, brands and sub-brands or take the reader rigorously through the process of distillation and the rituals of appreciation.

But no-one, as far as I know, has taken a look at Scotch as a brand – or more strictly speaking as an uber-brand. Individual brands, like Glenfiddich or Glenmorangie have their brand essence, positioning statements and values just like any other contemporary brand. But what about Scotch itself? And what about Scotch today, post-devolution, when Scotland itself is fighting off the shackles of hackneyed imagery and icons handed down from the Victorian age and forging a new identity and re-assessing its cultural values?

Tartan and bagpipes, stags and ghillies, clansmen and regimental colours still sell well overseas – as that one billionth bottle and all that went before it bear witness. But such imagery no longer has the same thrall over the post-colonial UK youth market (enamoured with lagers, alcopops and white spirits divorced from their heritage such as gin, vodka and rum) believed by many marketers and anxious brand managers to be crucial to capture for the future of the spirit.

So there's a deck of paradoxes at the crux of Scotch today. It's selling like never before but also suffering an identity crisis. It still carries the shadow of the hard man of drink and yet, especially in the world of Scotch Malt Whisky, restraint, moderation and responsible drinking are repeatedly emphasised. It's perceived by many as a masculine drink but stars like Madonna are partial to it, and Monica has been seen with a bottle of Glenmorangie on the set of *Friends*. It's perceived by many also as a dad's solo drink or night-cap but – even though one might ask where's the harm in that – there's more evidence of the conviviality of the spirit than ever before, with whisky festivals, sports, arts and community sponsorships, group tastings, visitor centres, whisky cruises and whisky trails galore.

This book sets out to try to shed some light on these paradoxes and to ask what is the brand essence of Scotch. Many writers from Burns to Iain Banks have written about Scotch and said some telling things and maybe the unofficial answer already lies in the writings of poets and sages and simply needs to be extracted. And distilled. But there's also the new question of a new Scotland and how Scotland sees itself now, five years after devolution.

Yes, Scotch Whisky is a world. There are many doors into that world. Come with me through a less travelled portal with regards to this world – the imagination.

A SUPERB SMWS MALT. CHRIS MILLER AND SUSANNA FREEDMAN'S 'CONTROVERSIAL' LABEL FOR 26 MALTS.

THE SKIPPABLE INTRO

Some interesting facts about Scotch Whisky

(Courtesy of the Scotch Whisky Association)

THE MARKET

Scotch Whisky outsells every other spirit in world markets.

More than 2,500 brands of Scotch Whisky are sold all over the world, of which as many as 200 are available in the home market. Many of them are sold only locally or to private clubs and individuals.

Scotch Whisky is one of Britain's principal export products, earning large amounts of foreign currency each year. Exporting is nothing new to the industry; even at the end of the nineteenth century Scotch Whisky companies were marketing overseas. Today, exports represent around 90 per cent of all Scotch Whisky sales.

As the country's most consistently successful export, Scotch Whisky makes a substantial net contribution to Britain's foreign exchange earnings and to companies' profits. Scotch Whisky is one of the UK's top five export earners.

In recent years, Scotch has been exported to about 200 different markets all over the world. The major markets are the European Union, the US and Japan and other Asian markets.

Sales to member states of the EU other than the UK are worth almost 40 per cent of exports. If the UK is included, the EU accounts for over 50 per cent of the total sales of Scotch Whisky.

In 2004:

- Malt whisky exports rose 15 per cent

- China entered the top 20 markets for the first time

- The US was the most valuable market, up three per cent to £338m

- 953 million bottles of Scotch Whisky were exported

- Scotch Malt Whisky exports soared worldwide, with over 55 million bottles of malt shipped.

Bottled malt whisky exports grew by 15 per cent in value compared with the previous year, topping £350m globally for the first time. The volume of bottled-in-Scotland malt whisky sent overseas grew by 12 per cent (6.1m bottles), with bottled blends also up one per cent (9.2m bottles).

Exports broke the £2bn barrier for the 12th year in succession.

WHAT IS SCOTCH WHISKY?

Scotch Whisky is a distillate made in Scotland from the elements of cereals, water and yeast.

A blended Scotch Whisky is a blend of as many as 50 individual Scotch malt and Scotch grain whiskies. Blended whiskies account for 95 per cent of all Scotch Whisky sold in world markets.

Most distilleries produce Scotch Whisky primarily for the purpose of blending, but many retain some of their production for sale as single whiskies. A single malt whisky is the product of one malt whisky distillery and a single grain whisky is the product of one grain whisky distillery.

Scotch Whisky has been defined in UK law since 1909 and recognised in European Community legislation since 1989. The current UK legislation relating specifically to Scotch Whisky is The Scotch Whisky Act 1988.

For the purposes of The Scotch Whisky Act 1988 "Scotch Whisky" means whisky:

(a) which has been produced at a distillery in Scotland from water and malted barley, with the addition of whole grains of other cereals only, and which has been:

(i) processed at that distillery into a mash;

(ii) converted to a fermentable substrate only by endogenous enzyme systems; and

(iii) fermented only by the addition of yeast.

(b) which has been distilled at an alcoholic strength by volume of less than 94.8 per cent so that the distillate has an aroma and taste derived from the raw materials used in, and the method of, its production;

AN OZARK MOUNTAIN OAK –
FIRST FILL BOURBON

(c) which has been matured in an excise warehouse in Scotland in oak casks of a capacity not exceeding 700 litres, the period of that maturation being not less than three years;

(d) which retains the colour, aroma and taste derived from the raw materials used in, and the method of, its production and maturation, and to which no substance other than water and spirit caramel has been added.

The Scotch Whisky Act 1988 prohibits inter alia the production in Scotland of whisky other than Scotch Whisky.

The Scotch Whisky Act 1988 and The European Spirits Definition Regulation both specify a minimum alcoholic strength of 40 per cent by volume, which applies to all Scotch Whisky bottled and/or put up for sale within or exported from the EU.

A blended Scotch Whisky is a blend of a number of distillates, each of which separately is entitled to the description "Scotch Whisky".

The period for which any blended Scotch Whisky is regarded as having been matured is that of the most recently distilled of the spirits contained in the blend.

There are around one hundred pot still malt distilleries and grain, or patent still, distilleries in Scotland; but the number working can vary from year to year.

Scotch Whisky can only be made in Scotland. Many other products which were originally manufactured only in a particular locality have lost their geographical significance and can now be manufactured anywhere. The word "Scotch", however, as applied to whisky, has retained its geographical significance. This is widely recognised in law throughout the world. Thus, whisky may be described as Scotch Whisky only if it has been wholly distilled and matured in Scotland.

The aim of the blender is first to produce a whisky of a definite and recognisable character. It is of the greatest importance that the blend should never vary from this standard. The second aim is, therefore, to achieve consistency.

ONE OF TALISKER'S WAREHOUSES. THESE CASKS WERE LAID DOWN IN 1973,
SO THE MALT HAS PROBABLY BEEN BOTTLED BY NOW.

The combining of malt with malt or grain with grain is known as vatting.

A deluxe blended whisky is a blend that contains a higher proportion of carefully selected older and, therefore, more expensive whiskies.

The law requires that when the age is declared on a label, it must refer to the youngest whisky in the blend. For example, if a blend is described as an eight-year-old, the youngest whisky in that blend must have been matured for at least eight years.

Scotch Whisky is not entitled to be described as Scotch Whisky until it has matured for three years. This does not apply to compounded spirits such as gin, vodka and liqueurs.

The normal practice is for the blender to buy the whisky as soon as it is distilled. It is then kept under bond in warehouses at the distillery to mature until the blender requires it. By law, whisky must mature for a minimum of three years, although in practice the minimum age is much greater. After blending, Scotch Whisky is usually returned to cask and left for a further period of several months to allow the constituent whiskies to "marry". It is then bottled for sale.

When distilled, Scotch is usually reduced for filling into casks at a strength of 63.5 per cent of alcohol by volume. The minimum bottling strength is 40 per cent alcohol by volume. Forty three per cent is often found in export markets, with occasional upward variations. The usual bottling strengths of other alcoholic drinks compares as:

- Cognac, rum   40 per cent
- Vodka, gin   37.5 per cent
- Fortified wine   20 per cent
- Champagne   13.1 per cent
- Table wines   11 per cent
- Beer   3.13 to 5.18 per cent

(Percentage of alcohol content by volume.)

WHISKY STOCKS

In 1939, the stocks of Scotch were 374 million litres of pure alcohol, but by the end of the war they had fallen to less than 247 million litres. Since then, they have grown in response to demand and by 1996 had risen more than tenfold to 2,741 million litres. Stocks of mature and maturing whisky are now sufficient to cover projected sales for almost nine years.

Financing stocks of maturing whisky is the most significant capital investment that Scotch Whisky companies have to undertake. The long period of maturation that Scotch Whisky must undergo poses a number of commercial problems. Not the least among these is the difficulty of forecasting accurately the demand for whisky several years ahead – which blenders must do when deciding how much new whisky to buy in any one season.

TAXATION AND DISCRIMINATION

Taxation in the UK is extremely high, accounting for as much as 70 per cent of the retail price of a typical bottle of standard blended Scotch Whisky. (Take away the tax and a 70cl bottle of blended Scotch Whisky would cost around £3.50.)

This includes value added tax, which is levied on the total retail price, including excise duty – a tax on a tax. The remainder of the retail price goes towards production and storage costs, transport, advertising, selling, administration expenses and wholesale and retail profits. The Government is thus by far the biggest beneficiary.

The excise duty paid on mature spirits is the same, whether they are produced in this country or abroad. Scotch Whisky is not protected in any way against competition from spirits produced overseas, even those from countries that themselves discriminate against imports of Scotch Whisky.

At the same time, Scotch Whisky is now much more heavily taxed than most competing drinks. Scotch Whisky therefore faces discrimination when competing in the UK market against other alcoholic drinks.

Excise duty has only been reduced on three occasions since the last century. The first cut was made in 1973. On that occasion, however, the rate was lowered only to compensate for the extra taxation that resulted from the introduction of value added tax, and made no difference to the overall impact.

A WOODCUT DEPICTING ILLICIT DISTILLERS AT WORK

During the following 20 years, more than once there had been reductions in the duty on high strength wines such as sherry and port, on sparkling wines, and on British wines made largely from imported grape juice.

However, in 1995 there was the first cut in tax on Scotch Whisky for one hundred years. There was a further cut in 1996. Although these cuts reduced the discrimination against Scotch Whisky slightly, it still carries a much greater tax burden than many of the drinks with which it competes in the market.

LOCAL EMPLOYMENT AND ECONOMIC IMPACT

Scotch Whisky is a prime example of a business cluster, supporting jobs not just in whisky companies but with local cereal suppliers, bottle and packaging manufacturers, transportation companies and suppliers of goods and services. One in 50 Scottish jobs – two per cent of all jobs – depends upon Scotch Whisky production. Many of these jobs are in economically fragile rural areas and disadvantaged urban areas. The economic impact of Scotch is considerable:

- The industry generates £800m of salaries in Scotland and £1.3bn in the UK

- It spends almost £700m on local goods and services in Scotland and over £1bn in the UK

- It spends £90m alone on purchasing cereals in Scotland

- Distillery visitor centres, whisky heritage centres and whisky trails attract around one million visitors to Scotland, further boosting the national and rural economies.

A COOPER'S ART – MAKING UP CASKS FROM STAVES.

THE TOP TEN MARKETS 2004

	Value	Volume (70cl bottles)
US	£337.9m	118.2m
Spain	£289.5m	111.9m
France	£245.2m	136.2m
South Korea	£125.2m	33.8m
Greece	£85.7m	26.9m
Taiwan	£82.3m	18.9m
Germany	£78.5m	36.3m
Japan	£61.6m	14.7m
Portugal	£55.4m	19.5m
Venezuela	£49.9m	24.9m

QUICK FACTS

Scotch Whisky accounts for more than 20 per cent of UK food and drink exports.

• Scotch Whisky sells nearly four times its nearest rival whisky.

• One in 50 Scottish jobs rely on the Scotch Whisky industry.

• Some 18.5 million casks lie maturing in warehouses in Scotland.

• Greeks drink more Scotch Whisky per person than any other nation.

• More Scotch is sold in one month in France than cognac in a year.

• In Spain, they mix it with cola and drink it out of wooden bowls.

• Research has shown that regular moderate drinking of alcohol, including Scotch Whisky, may provide protection from coronary heart disease.

• The "cup o' kindness" in Robert Burns' 'Auld Lang Syne' refers to Scotch Whisky, the spirit of friendship.

ANYTHING GOES

In olden days a glimpse of stocking Was looked on as something shocking, But now, God knows, Anything goes.

Cole Porter

Short, long, neat, mixed, on the rocks; guys, gals: there ain't no more shocks.

AFTER MACPHERSON

From the MacDougall Fragment, found in a cave
on the Isle of Islay, MMVIII

Shin an ceannard a chuach dhan duine og.
"Ol" ars esan
"Gu de a th'ann?" ars an duine og
"Is e sin uisge beatha."
"Tha fhios gu bheil cumhachd ann"
"Tha sin. Tha e giulain na tha de sgeoil
anns na reultan."

The chief passed the cup to the young man.
"Drink," he said.
"What is it?" asked the young man.
"It's the water of life."
"It must be strong."
"It is. It carries as many stories as the stars."

Translated from the Gaelic by Aonghas Macneacail.
Note: Uisge beatha is the Gaelic for "water of life";
the word whisky is derived from uisge, "uiskie".

EXACTLY. SARA SHERIDAN AND DAVID FREER'S 26 MALTS LABEL.

CHAPTER 1
2020
A MATTER
OF TASTE

Well show me the way
To the next whisky bar
Oh, don't ask why
Oh, don't ask why

The Doors

Lachlan Macallister feels younger today than he ever has. Silver haired and in his white suit and thistle-studded gold cravat he sits at his customary table, flanked by tall vases of red roses. In a short while he will be joined by his long time lover Emilia Sanchez. For her, this part of the city is uncharted territory. She's an artist and draws her inspiration from the shoreline upstate, where the Beat Poets partied and broke orange crates for firewood so many years ago. She has the card though – the name, John Damian's, like embossed iron on a background of russet vellum, a quartet of alchemical symbols marking the corners. Of course all the smart cab drivers know its whereabouts. The bar's as famous in the city today as Haight Ashbury was in the 60s. She'll find him. Challenge him too, no doubt, as to the choice of rendezvous. He will stand, pull back a copper-plated chair and, when she's seated, introduce her to this gleaming world. It's peopled by women as much as men. That will seem strange to her, as maybe it does to you. Don't speak. Not yet. Let us eavesdrop, here, on one regular foursome.

The aromatherapist, the fashion designer, the actress and the crime writer. They're all chic, will admit to an upper age limit of 32, and are all dressed to dance with the devil, or "the de'il" as Lachlan would say with a trace of Hebridean lilt still in his voice. Lavish gear has become de rigueur in this magician's cavern. Their rings and chokers sparkle in the candlelight reflected from the swan-like curves of the copper walls. The Latin waiter sets down the tray of aperitifs. These are on the house and come in addition to the bowls of salted cashews and glistening olives: John Damian's has impeccable style. The ritual begins – Giselle, the aromatherapist, places a tulip-shaped glass in front of each of her friends then takes the brass decanter (that reminds the onlooker somewhat of the opium pipe his father brought back from India) and pours each a generous dram of the establishment's "malt of the moment".

They swirl the golden spirit in the glass. Vibeke's fingers are plumper than Giselle's and Su-Li's are naturally darker – Chase wears lace and leather gloves (she says she writes in ink) – but each gives an accomplished, elegant twirl before holding their glass to the light. Today, the spirit seems to hold its translucent contour up beneath the rim of the glass, before tears begin to break away and slowly descend to rejoin the body of malt. Tears, church windows, legs ... as we shall see, the language of whisky is as rich and varied and as fluid as the substance it describes. The Scottish grandee, or whoever he is – whisky ambassador, writer or sleuth, rumours abound but there's no consensus – calls them Tara's tears. But, before we move on, the viscous tears denote an oiliness and a malt high in alcoholic content. Our four have clocked that and are swapping caution with bravado, declamation with pregnant pause. The night is young. And they haven't touched a drop.

Nor will they, for a while. If fact, you could be forgiven, if you weren't a native of San Francisco and had stumbled across this bar as a refuge from the street jangle or early evening April rain, for thinking that you had entered an Arabesque perfumery. It's the nosing hour. And going by the contemplative utterances, sighs of pleasure and shrieks of laughter, it's a happy hour too. Chase has a nose as sharp as any of her fictional detectives. She's sniffing the mystery malt undiluted. That's the way: taking it neat first – a gingerly approach being best so as not to anaesthetise the nose – then adding a dash, followed by up to an equal amount of water, to awaken the spirit and release its inner secrets. The experts, back in Scotland, talk about aromas being intense, complex, forward or shy. Once, long ago he likened this sensory exploration to foreplay in a client's copy. An account executive, having herself laughed, excised it. Rightly, Lachlan's sure. But listen now to our foxy ladies. Searching, investigating: a bit of a tussle.

They're at the neat stage:

"It's like the breeze off the sea at Monterrey Bay."

"Big Sur – with a tinge of wood smoke."

"I don't smell the wood smoke. It's too fresh."

"Yes, like ... like cucumber, or dill."

"I said a tinge."

BOTTLE CELLO. KATE PATRICK AND RON BURNETT'S LOVELY 26 MALTS LABEL.
EVEN THE MANDATORIES ARE BEAUTIFULLY CRAFTED.

"Giselle smells a tinge of wood smoke."

"A hint."

"I like hint." Su-Li, not Chase. She's the fashion designer.

"There's a warmth. A quiet confidence. It's not overpowering."

"Instantly likeable."

They all nod.

"Vanilla."

A communal mmmm.

"Fudge."

"Vanilla fudge. Is there vanilla fudge?"

"'Course."

"There's a herb in there."

"Hey, Big Sur."

"Nah. Fennel."

"Uh uh," says Vibeke, "Liquorice, aniseed, fennel – hate them all."

"So?"

"If that was in there, I couldn't agree to instantly likeable."

"Tarragon!"

"That's it!"

Now Giselle takes the jug of water. She pours. Open sesame.

"Wow!"

"That's strong!"

"Acrid!"

"No, more, more ..."

"A sea cavern."

"Lady's jockstrap."

"Chase!"

"More water."

Splash. They drink. They let it rest on the tongue. No novices here. Oily liquid from the lips to the well of the throat.

"It's rude."

"Hot."

"Fiery."

"The fire comes out in the water."

"There's smoke now; peat."

"It's gotta be Islay."

"It's deceptive."

"Janus."

"Jekyll and Hyde."

"Two sisters."

"One tame, one wild."

"Embers on sand."

"It rides the waves."

"Burning oil on water."

"Once over the shock, hooked," says Vibeke, swallowing.

"Angel's pee."

"Not angel's share!"

"No. Angel's pee. Divinely acrid."

"I don't agree with the acrid bit."

"One or more angels?"

"Depends where you put the apostrophe."

There's a clatter of glasses. A wreath of smiles. The evening has begun. The world of whisky has been entered by one of countless doors. Now they call for the waiter: "Antonio! Antonio!" It may not be his real name. But it's what he answers to at John Damian's. The "girls" call for their favourite brands. These they'll drink long. In fact, Antonio already has a tray loaded. Highball glasses crammed with ice. Bottles of Scotch from the ice cave of a fridge that lines the back of the bar. Coke, ginger beer, arctic water. After the fire of their Islay aperitif, the appearance of chilled glass and ice along with the golden whisky and tra-la-la mixers is most welcome. And Antonio pours with panache, holding the bottle a good six inches from the lip of the glass and letting the whisky flow as from a fountain. Optics? As they say over here: they're history.

CRAFTED WHISKY, CRAFTED LABEL, CRAFTY BRAND.

Chase is a Compass Box devotee – Peat Monster or Hedonism topping her bill. For Giselle, if it's malt it's likely to be Glenfiddich's Doe-Eyed Jo,[1] or if it's a blend, Johnnie Walker's Red Lady. Su-Li is enchanted by wood (ah, wood – we'll return to wood): Balvenie and Glenmorangie are her favourite distilleries; lately Kaildon is her tipple, even though, strictly speaking purists still eschew it as part of the 2017 Juniper Heresy. For Vibeke, Highland Park 12 Year Old: Preacher's Silence always does the trick, a gale mellowed in sherry and heather. Brands have come a long way. To think that once half the adult market was virtually uncatered for by the Scotch Whisky industry! When of all the spirits this is the one with the most subtlety and variety of taste, the one with the most exotic, elusive and alluring fan of scents – in other words, the most sensually appealing: the feminine domain. But, as the radicals say – cut the crap: it tastes good. Lachlan? Well, The Macallan's Rooster Dandy is always welcome but today he has a Laphroaig 10 Year Old: same as it ever was. Horses for courses: a market in bloom.

Julienne, the proprietor, catches Lachlan's eye. Emilia has arrived, as raven-haired as Lady Macbeth[2] but with dark Iberian eyes, not the sky blue of the northern Celt. Yes, the latter day whisky baron signals, bring the champagne. (Emilia Sanchez is not a convert to whisky, you'll have gathered.) Champagne, cognac and armagnac are all great drinks and are distinctive too in that they bear the name of their provenance. But let me tell you the story of Scotch, the only drink the world over that bears the name of its nation.

1. Jo – In Scots, joy or term of endearment, sweetheart, lover; as in Robert Burns' "John Anderson, my jo".

2. Macbeth in Gaelic means "son of life". Ironic, yes. But actually he was a good king. Shakespeare has led us to believe otherwise.

CHAPTER 2
1963–1977
FIRST
ENCOUNTERS

As far as I can recall, my first conscious encounter with whisky was in *The Crab with the Golden Claws*, the Tintin adventure in which the eponymous, strangely coiffured hero meets Captain Haddock for the first time. Haddock is blootered (or mingin, stottin, steamin,[1] mortal, fou as a puggie,[2] to use a few good Scots words) caterwauling about his mummy. The source of his inebriation is a bottle of golden liquid bearing a pillar-box red label marked "Old Whisky" in bold black type.

The captain's unhappy of course. His ship has been taken over by bandits. Or maybe his ship was an easy target because of his little problem. Either way, once he gets in tow with Tintin, and his dog Snowy, in the endless fight against baddies from every corner of the globe he becomes a reformed character – with relapses.

Captain Haddock added a bit of fire and guts and human fallibility to the goody-two-shoes and rather anodyne Tintin. I like to think the whisky had a bit to do with that.

As Raymond Chandler said, " ... a man ought to get drunk at least twice a year just on principle, so he won't let himself get snotty about it." And that, readers from today's industry with its noble and correct stance on responsible drinking, I found in *The Scotch Whisky Industry Record* by H. Charles Craig. Ostensibly a dry, encyclopaedic tome, it's actually a great read with some wonderful anecdotes. The fact is you can't write a book about as strong a drink as whisky without mentioning drunkenness. It wouldn't be irresponsible; it would be blind. Show me the man or woman from the industry who disagrees with Chandler and I'll show you the door to the fairy kingdom. Whisky's a tiger.

It's also a great survivor. Distilleries have come and gone, brands have come and gone, personal fortunes have been made and lost, but as an uber-brand, Scotch Whisky has survived legislation, persecution and prohibition. It's surviving the onslaught of white spirits and squibs such as alcopops. It can take just about anything that's

A 1970S WHYTE & MACKAY LABEL, JUST AS I REMEMBER IT.

thrown at it. So read on, undaunted. Relax, in fact. Pour yourself another dram. And, like the girls in John Damian's, kick off those shoes.

My dad, of course, drank whisky. I say of course because, broadly speaking, he was in the colonial mindset, working abroad for stints in various British embassies. So whisky and water or whisky and soda was a ritual sun downer, alternating with gin and tonic. My mum drank it too.

One of my early memories – not from equatorial heat but from temperate Surrey – is of the patriarchal goodnight kiss with a waft of whisky and water and pickled onions. Whyte & Mackay, with its red lion label, was the brand I remember – standing on the larder shelf among the cluster of spirits. That was before the drinks cupboard was established. Before he discovered malts.

My father became a collector of malts long before it became fashionable and was an early member of the Scotch Malt Whisky Society. I'm still trying to track down his membership number, but it pre-dates computer records. Somewhere, in a musty file, will be a typed letter with his signature: the energetic scratch in blue ink fading.

At a certain age, my brothers and I were offered the pre-prandial Scotch (Teachers or Claymore, if not Whyte & Mackay) with water and ice: a long cold drink in a squat tumbler; a long cold drink with a circling coil of golden fire. Thinking back, it strikes me that it wasn't Haig's. We all went to the same school as Earl Haig, where his statue, heavy in field marshal's trench coat, dominates the promenade, and my father didn't exactly think kindly of school. He certainly didn't want to recall it at six o'clock every evening. For by his own account he was beaten regularly, hoicked onto a prefect's back and whacked angrily and senselessly in the echoing church-like vastness of the building known as Big School. And he was sent home for good after catching pneumonia on a corps exercise. A good development as it so happened: he finished his education under private tutelage in Paris, where he acquired a taste for hedonism and learnt to make the perfect cocktail. Strange that he sent his sons to the same establishment. Of course, it was much more lenient in my day. I bought my Che Guevara poster and bundle of joss sticks from a prefect on my first night, after "prayers". And that set the tone for the next four years.

In 1973, I went on a pre-university art appreciation course to Venice, Florence and Rome and it was in Venice, in a pensione by the Academia Bridge that I recall first seeing a bottle of malt. The rather whey-faced boy I was sharing a room with had a, what is now iconic, triangular bottle of Glenfiddich. (Ergonomically designed, according to apocryphal accounts, by the brother of the King of Sweden.) This was ten years after William Grant and Sons had taken one of the boldest steps in the history of Scotch Whisky: releasing a single malt Scotch Whisky onto the market for public consumption. It was a visionary step, which in time has come to create a whole other dimension to the uber-brand and Glenfiddich remains the world's top-selling malt whisky brand. Forty years on, the whisky world, mirroring creation and the scientific theory of possible worlds, is a house with many mansions. How I'd like to be able to write to my

THE TIMELESS GLENMORANGIE 10 YEAR OLD LABEL – HARDLY CHANGED SINCE ROBIN HARDIE'S BOTTLE.

father, tell him of the many doors, wickets and posterns and maybe draw him a map of this brave new world that there was but an inkling of in his twilight.

At Oxford, I came across my first bottle of Glenmorangie, Scotland's top selling malt brand. I lived with a band of mild subversives in a wonderful Gothic house in leafy North Oxford, just round the corner from J. R. R. Tolkien's old house, where I imagined him writing the Father Christmas Letters, which had just been posthumously released the year before.

For me this context is significant, for Oxford helped shape my imagination probably more, even, than my intellect. Although, having said that, discussing with my philosophy tutor the difference between a glass being half full and half empty will always remain a seminal moment in understanding language. What I should have said, of course, was, "It depends on the drink sir. With whisky, the glass is always half empty."

But alongside the questioning is the dreaming. And Oxford is a matrix of spiritual fantasy, particularly in its winter cocoon, with hidden kingdoms and possibilities leading off snow-muffled, lamp-lit streets. It's not difficult to see how the imaginations of C. S. Lewis, Charles Williams and Philip Pullman as well as Tolkien were, in part, shaped by this city. Lewis Carroll and Alice, I always think, along with *Brideshead Revisited* and *Three Men in a Boat*, is Oxford in summer.

And it was in North Oxford, in summer, in the downstairs bedroom that led on to the wooden veranda with steps down into the walled garden that I came across Robin Hardie's bottle of Glenmorangie Ten Years Old. Robin, a Scot as his surname suggests, was a long-stay guest who had scored marks with a black biro down the label. Charting his nips? Mmm. That's not what his hosts and friends thought.

His proprietary stance was, however, quite unnecessary. None of us touched the stuff. We were virtually tee-total! And it was interesting that the "greenery" we transplanted from the said walled garden to Wytham Woods[3] for safe-keeping, fell – in Robin's mind, having accompanied us on the expedition – into the category of "share and share alike".

That's the power of a brand over home-grown for you: it gives the stuff it garnishes tangible, recognisable value. To be fair to Robin, ten years later when my fiancée and I camped for a six months stint in his spare bedroom in Clapham, the room was lined with box upon box of superb, specially imported Chilean wine, and when we viewed it in the same category as the Wytham greenery Robin never batted an eyelid.

My first real immersion into the world of malt whisky was playing poker with my father and three brothers. My dad always had his malts straight in satisfyingly solid little shot glasses. That meant we followed suit. It was years later that I learnt the efficacy and orthodoxy of adding water. When it was the turn of Bourbon, we had it on the rocks. The Scotch was manly, the Bourbon was desperado-cool. The malts I remember were Jura, Fettercairn and Old Pulteney. Jura,[4] pale in colour, delicate on the nose, slightly oily, with a hint of peat was my favourite. Sweet and estery Fettercairn with traces of fudge. (Charlie MacLean, one of today's leading whisky writers, indicates that Fettercairn leaves a very slight rubbery taste on the back of the tongue: his notes and sensory accuracy bring this malt back to mind, for I haven't tasted it since those Somerset nights of cigar haze and sibling merriment.) Pulteney with notes of almond, marzipan and lemon sherbet marks that time too. The time of first loves and leaving home.

1. The temperance reformers had a paddle-steamer, *The Ivanhoe*, which provided excursions on the River Clyde from 1880 to compete with the steam boats that were notorious as floating boozers. Steam boats were not covered by the 1853 prohibition on the selling of alcohol on the Sabbath (thus "steaming" as the popular Scots term for drunken).

2. Puggie – a monkey.

3. Wytham Woods is the University's privately-owned woods used for research by various scientific disciplines. The woods, with their great ancient roots and sense of peace, were also the inspiration for the elven woods of Lostloriel in *The Lord of the Rings*.

4. I remember the lightness of Jura which now, having visited the island several times, seems somewhat at odds with such a brooding, atmospheric place – though a blazing summer afternoon spent in the delightful walled gardens of Jura House is etched in my memory as a perfect summer's day. That's the Scottish islands for you. One day you can imagine you're basking in the Aegean, the next that the Nordic Gods of the Wind and the Rain have got it in for you and every other poor sod on the island.

CHAPTER 3
2020
JOHN BARLEYCORN IS DEAD

After a while, when her eyes have adjusted from the brightness of the beach to the gold and amber hues of the bar, when she's taken a sip from her flute and let the bubbles infect her, when she's countered her disdain for the nature of the venue with admiration at its splendour, when she's told Lachlan of her day and the jewels of light she's glimpsed, when she's enquired after his health and gauged the tone of his bonhomie and enquired whether they'd be staying in town or heading up state to his ocean-side cabin, she indicates she is all ears – in fact, she says, she'll go so far as to say she wants to know, tonight, the secrets of the barley. But first, she's intrigued by the centrepiece of the room: a glass case, roofed and rimmed with bright metal, housing silver and chrome mechanicals with shutters, hinges and spouts and a steady flow of liquid passing through.

"It's a spirit safe," says Lachlan. "Or, more exactly, a simulation of one."

"It's beautiful. What's it for?"

"It's where the cut of the distillate is made." She hears nothing that has meaning. The complexity of whisky is exactly why it needs poetry. And patience. Or simply receptive taste buds. But there's more to life than the senses.

"It's where the alchemy takes place."

"Yes, it looks like a chamber of transformations."

"In the debatable land between science and art."

"You tell me."

"We're jumping ahead of ourselves."

"That we mustn't do." She smiles into her Moët.

"We'll kick off with single malt."

"Why single? Sounds lonely."

"Single means the product of one distillery and one distillery only."

"Ah, rugged individuals."

"Precisely. We start with barley."

"Blowing gold in the bracing Scottish wind."

"It doesn't have to be Scottish. Just good."

"Gold."

"Gold," Lachlan nods, quietly. Then he takes an old-fashioned nib pen from his inside breast pocket, unscrews the cap and begins to write on the paper table cloth (an inspired touch of John Damian's, allowing the imbibers to scribble their thoughts and responses with boldness and immediacy). The gold nib allows for a thick flowing script.

Barley
↓
Water
↓
Fire (peat)
↓
GBH
↓
Steam
↓
Heart
↓
Wood
↓
Time (hours and hours and hours)
↓
Nectar

"Hours and hours and hours – sounds like Van Morrison. And GBH?"

"Grievous bodily harm."

"Ouch."

"I'll explain."

"In the taxi," she says, setting aside the glasses and rolling up the table cloth like a general might roll up a field map.

"I'm glad it ends in nectar," she says. "Glad for the barley. Glad for the man or woman."

As they speed north of the city along the coast, gradually leaving the lights trailing behind like jewels flung by a fleeing thief, she nestles in to his chest, the sound of the Pacific to her left, the sound of his voice leading her on a virtual tour of an Atlantic-facing distillery in far-away Scotland, to her right. He chooses a coastal distillery purposely. Of the hundred odd distilleries in Scotland (not all of them in operation, some of them being "mothballed" as the charming euphemism for current inertia describes them) only a handful are by the sea. But he likes the symmetry his and Emilia's present proximity to the ocean provides. He likes the symbolism of the ocean too. Here, the context is trade. Trade on a grand scale, steeped in history and adventure. The story of Scotch, an extraordinarily successful export from a small, often misunderstood, country on the outer fringe of its proud and confident continent. It's not a story that can be told in one night. And tomorrow his lover's ears will be distracted by other calls: the seagulls' caw; wind in driftwood. This night he wants her to catch a glimpse of the spirit itself, unburdened by history and all the razzmatazz. Unburdened, too, by the ins and outs of manufacture. But to set the scene of transformation he must first, albeit impressionistically, describe the alchemist's workshop.

"Crossing the water you lose all sense of time. Especially when the sea is calm. Like today. Except for the cutting of the ocean by the ferry's prow and the occasional porpoise arcing, it's like twinkling glass. Care seems to fall away, like drops of spray tumbling back into the surf.

"The port is tiny. A hotel, a shop, a bus shelter, a few harbour sheds, a lifeboat station – at least that's how it was when last I went that way.

"We drive off, passing the clutch of cars and backpackers waiting for the small roll-on roll-off that heads east to Jura. Up the steep bank and onto the island's plateau. Then before long we turn right down what's little more than a track."

"Where are you taking me?" she murmurs.

"Past a gleaming building of glass and chrome."

"What is it?"

"A distillery."

"Ah."

"But we don't stop. We keep going to the end of the track. We're met by a man with a pig."

"A farmer?"

"He's the distillery manager."

"Is this 2020?"

"This is 2020. But not in the story. When we were younger."

"When the world was less sophisticated ..."

"Yes."

"And distillery managers had pigs."

"Well, this one did."

"I like that. I'll drink his whisky."

"You'd like his whisky – as an easy malt or in one of the smoother blends. The distillery has an earthy feel for all its pagodas and look of a garrison or outpost. It's unpretentious, a place of work,

LAGAVULIN DISTILLERY. ISLAY. THE SPIRITUAL HOME OF WHITE HORSE.

immaculately clean. But it has a view to die for. Beyond the jetty there's a beach, some cottages, a headland, a rusting hull and, across the sound, rising majestically the Paps of Jura."

"Breasts?"

"That's what they're called. There are three of them."

"A witch's."

"Beautiful in the sunshine, brooding in the rain. But now Hamish leads us inside."

"Hamish?"

"The distillery manager."

"The man with the pig."

"The pig stays outside."

Lachlan then tells Emilia of the lay-out of the distillery. It's designed around a process like any factory. But never was there a factory, whether it was for bicycles or biscuits, that felt so organic, that hummed so quietly, that smelt so good, that looked so mysterious. As he begins to describe the different spaces, the barn floors, the receptacles, the mill, the tubs, the copper pipes, he begins also to tell the barley's story. He's whispering now. They've not far to go. He can see the storm lights of his cabin on the headland. In the dark, it could be Scotland. In her incipient, sliding dream it surely is. He tells her how two great Scottish poets, Robert Burns and, more recently George Mackay Brown, both described the making of whisky from the barley's point of view: John Barleycorn. He lives and breathes and feels. He almost dies. But not quite. His shell is stripped, his body's crushed. But his spirit is released. This is a story of transformation.

"There were three kings into the east/Three kings both great and high," starts Burns' poem.

"And they hae sworn a solemn oath/John Barleycorn should die." The barley is harvested. In both poems it's presumed dead. But there's rebirth. A long journey awaits these golden ears.

The barley arrives at the distillery. It's steeped in water for five days. This is to start a germination process, to break down the protein and release the starch. From the starch will come sugar; from sugar, the alcohol.

"No jumping ahead." She's hanging on. He breathes in the perfume of her hair.

"Then, traditionally," he continues, "the wet barley – green malt as it's now called – is laid out on the distillery's barn floors and painstakingly turned and turned before being laid on a rack to be dried by the heat from a kiln. Only a handful of distilleries do that any more."

"Heroes."

"Yes. But, you know, the pressures of commerce..."

"Blah, blah ... what happens to John next?"

"Well, if you want smoky whisky, you put peat in the kiln."

"Is he a friend of John's?"

"Sssh. John is now malted barley and he's ground in a mill and turned into grist. He can hardly recognise himself. All they want from him is his starch. The grist is then transferred into large mash tubs where it's mixed with hot water around 63.50 centigrade. It's here the starch converts to sugar."

"Tubs?"

"Yes."

"Tubs could be a cat."

"Distilleries usually do have cats – ratters and mousers – but we're talking big wooden tubs here. There are two types of tubs used in the process. The mash tubs and then what are called the wash backs.

"Now, when the starch converts to sugar it's called worts."

"Poor John. What ignominy."

"Yeast is added to the worts in the wash backs and fermented into a beery alcohol around seven or eight per cent. This is a dramatic part of the journey for John Barleycorn – he's jigged about and froths up. He goes through yet more changes with fruity compounds called esters being produced. What we now have is called the wash.

"I'll give you an idea of how big these tubs are. During World War II, the Highland Park distillery on Orkney went 'dark': it stopped making whisky. But it helped the war effort in an unusual way. There were about 60,000 British troops stationed on the island, and the soldiers who were billeted near the distillery used the wash backs as bath tubs. The tubs measure some 12 feet across and 18 feet deep, so it's easy to imagine a whole platoon per wash back."

"Appropriately named then. You scratch my back ..." She sighs and stretches, slinky and light against his body. "So how is this ugly duckling, this green malt cum grist cum wort cum wash transformed into nectar?"

"Well we're now ready for the purification – the distilling itself. The still room, at first glance, gives an impression of a Moorish city, with the gleaming copper stills like the domes of mosques and palaces."

"Like John Damian's!"

"Exactly."

Lachlan realises that the taxi has been stationary for a while. He looks out of the window. They are home; as much as anywhere outside his native Scotland can be called home. He's aware that his romanticisation of his subject owes much to a low-lying homesickness: a condition shared by many expatriate Scots, not only of first or second generation but indeed of the older diaspora that numbered at least eight to every one left back in the auld country. The accent might be lost but the blood is haunted. And for every whisky-loving ex-pat there is a splash of nostalgia in the amber.

He shakes himself and looks at the driver, whose head is inclined, whose ears are cocked. He too is waiting to hear the end of the story.

"Have you turned off the meter?" asks Lachlan.

"Yes sir," says the driver.

"OK. The wash is now boiled up twice in copper stills. The copper helps create certain flavours and remove unwanted compounds. This is the distillation. The wash is vaporised at the top of the stills and as the steam comes back down it returns to liquid form: spirit. The spirit goes through the spirit-safe where the purest part or 'the cut' is taken and the rest drained away. What we now have is 'new make spirit'. JB feels light, clean, reborn; if a bit raw.

"The worst is over. The new make spirit is transferred to casks or barrels that have had a previous fill of either sherry or Bourbon and have been specially prepared and fired by coopers. The treatment of wood and indeed the choice of wood is now recognised as playing a major part in the production of whisky ..."

THE STILLS AT CRAGGANMORE

"Oh yeah," pipes up the driver, "I remember all that controversy over those guys using olive and ash wood and ..."

"The Juniper Heresy, yes – it's interesting but I must finish now. Once the casks are filled, they are rolled into the warehouse and racked. They lie there for many years allowing the whisky to slowly mature and grow in complexity and depth of flavour. People talk about the whisky resting now

THE SPIRIT SAFE AT GLENMORANGIE

but actually there's a lot of chemical activity taking place between the spirit and the wood. But for John Barleycorn the pain is over."

"Maybe his dreams are vivid, sir – with the occasional nightmare as his unconscious revisits the flaying or the milling or that vicious bath tub."

"Yes," says Lachlan, connecting his transactor to the taxi's pay terminal. "And as time goes by John Barleycorn feels richer and silkier. He smells wonderful and tastes divine and, in the words of George Mackay Brown, is ready to 'flush the winters of men with wassails of corn.'"

"And women too," murmurs Emilia.

"And angels."

"Angels?"

"Yes, a certain amount of the spirit evaporates during its time in the warehouse and the lost whisky is known as the angels' share."

"The ones into jazz. John Coltrane."

Her eyelids fall softly on her high cheekbones for the final time that night. Transaction complete and the driver tipped off with the name of an unsurpassed Glenrothes Vintage, Lachlan steps out into the starlight, his raven lover in his arms.

CHAPTER 4
1494
AND NOT AN EDINBURGH ADVERTISING AGENCY IN SIGHT[1]

The earliest records of distillation go back as far as 7000 BC. China, Abyssinia and Egypt are all contenders for the honour of originator. I even glimpsed somewhere – trawling the internet – a claim that the oldest still in the world had been found in Mongolia. What seems certain is that the Arabs perfected the secrets of distilling around the tenth century, the process being first used to create perfume. So Lady Macbeth, running barefoot across the flagstones at Dunsinane, circa 1017, could quite legitimately have known about the perfumes of Arabia and called on their penetrative, masking powers to sweeten her guilty little hand. What we don't know for sure is whether she would have been able to steady her nerves with a primitive brew of whisky. Certainly, the Arab refinements wouldn't have reached Scotland by that time. And these refinements were without doubt pivotal. For as every devotee knows, the connection between distilling and aroma is of particular significance to

EARLY DISTILLERS WITH TONSURES.

whisky, for whisky of all the world's distillates flourishes in the domain of scent.

Trade may seem the obvious way by which the knowledge came from one culture to another. But who knows, it may have been a prize won in the Crusades, maybe as ransom for a musk and jasmine scented Saracen in the Holy Land. Whatever the route, soon monasteries all over Europe were busy making distilled liquors, ostensibly for medicinal purposes. Legend has it that the art (or science) of distilling reached Scotland via Irish monks, following the trail of the Celtic Church founded by St Patrick and St Columba some centuries before. If this was the case, the island of Islay – lying within sight of Northern Ireland – would have been the most likely first port of call.

Standing on the pebbled beach at Kilchoman, down from the ruined chapel with its font and warrior graves, it's not hard to imagine a barque being hauled by monks onto the shingle, the primitive paraphernalia of alchemy safely stowed on board along with chalices, crucifixes and illuminated bibles. When I was briefed to write a 15-minute film script for the Bowmore visitor centre in 2002 I stood on that beach with friend and film maker Andy Hibbert and we painted such pictures on the wind.

Temporal rulers have always kept a wary eye on what privileges their spiritual peers are enjoying, so it's little wonder that the earliest Scottish record of aqua vitae is an entry in the Exchequer Rolls of Scotland of 1494: "eight bolls[2] of malt to Friar John Cor wherewith to make aqua vitae" for the king

(James IV). Friar John Cor was of the Benedictine Order at Lindores Abbey, near Newburgh in Fife. He sounds like he could have come straight out of Philip Pullman's *His Dark Materials*. But then James was looking for doors into other worlds. He was interested in alchemy – something else that also originated from Arabia (al kimia: the alloying of metals). In 1503, an entry in the Lord High Treasurer's Account states: "Item: for 5½ choppinis of aqua vitae to the curyes of quinta essentica, 11s." In other words, 5½ choppinis (whatever measure that was) of whisky to make the quintessence. The fifth essence being that which would turn base metal into gold. There are also records of aqua vitae being employed in the making of gunpowder – possibly to wet the mixture of saltpetre, sulphur and charcoal.

Around the same time, John Damian, the Abbot of Tungland was also attempting to make the quinta essentica. This essence remained elusive. And fifteenth-century Scots poet William Dunbar suggested that Damian's famous attempt to fly from the walls of Stirling Castle was not a stunt but a real attempt to escape from Scotland, his trials at making the quintessence, using gold and silver as well as whisky, having proved such an expensive flop. My colleague John Ormston came across this story when we were looking for stories of rare creatures, things and happenings when we launched our writing company Henzteeth in 2002. Along with the Northern Hairy Nosed Wombat, snow in the Sahara, a Druid's Egg and The Dunmow Bacon, we found The Birdman of Stirling.[3] At that time, we didn't know his proper name. I only came across it when researching this book. The 50-word vignette is by my colleague John; the design is by long-time collaborator Damian (Mullan). Spooky.

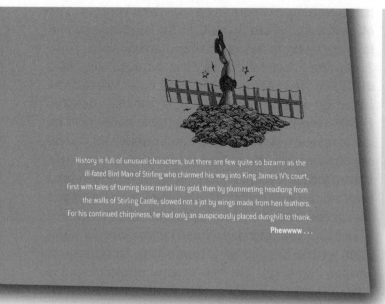

THE BIRDMAN OF STIRLING – HENZTEETH STATIONERY.

History is full of unusual characters, but there are few quite so bizarre as the ill-fated Bird Man of Stirling who charmed his way into King James IV's court, first with tales of turning base metal into gold, then by plummeting headlong from the walls of Stirling Castle, slowed not a jot by wings made from hen feathers. For his continued chirpiness, he had only an auspiciously placed dunghill to thank. Phewwww . . .

The power of the monasteries was, of course, soon to be dissolved. Many beautiful abbeys and priories were pillaged, bombarded and left to crumble; the treasures ended up at the Royal court (where else?) but the good news – for the secular world at least – was that the science (or art) of distillation passed from behind closed walls. By the 1570s, aqua vitae, or "uisge beatha" as it was known by the common folk in Scotland, was being widely drunk. Indeed, the knowledge passed from the monks to the farmers, which is not surprising since many monasteries had farms attached, and possibly many monks, on leaving their orders, took gainful employ under their long-time neighbours. Distilling took place on Morangie farm from the 1660s, and interestingly the nearby Royal Burgh of Tain had had a bishopric dating from the ninth century. The Macallan and Springbank are also famously known for once being modest farm distilleries.

But even before the farmers became the chief distillers the surgeon barbers had taken the secrets out of the monasteries. In 1505, a Seal of Cause was granted by the City of Edinburgh and confirmed by the king the following year, under which the Guild of Surgeon Barbers had a monopoly for the manufacture of aqua vitae. Another early record underscores this point: in 1556, one Bessie Campbell was commanded by the bailies of Edinburgh "to desist and cease from any further making of aqua vitae within this burgh". Interesting that it was a woman; as historian Tom Devine remarks in *The Scottish Nation: 1700–2000* there is a long tradition in Scotland of women making whisky – not always the most savoury of women.[4] The vignette in the footnote would pose a horrific image for today's marketers and brand architects.

But how was whisky perceived back then, before advertising as we know it? Raphael Holinshed, compiler of *The Chronicles of England, Scotland and Ireland* (1577) acclaimed the virtues and qualities of usquebaugh as follows. He starts with the qualifier, "Beying moderately taken", which resonates, of course, with every contemporary brand's website! *"Beying moderately taken it cutteth fleume, it lighteneth the mynd, it quickeneth the spirits, it cureth the hydropsie, it healeth the strangury,[5] it pounceth the stone, it repelleth gravel, it puffeth away ventositie, it kepyth and preserveth the hed from whirling, the eys from dazelying, the tongue from lispying, the mouth from snafflying, the teeth from chetterying, the throte from rattlying, the weasan from stieflying, the stomach from womblying, the harte from swellying, the bellie from wirtching, the guts from rumblying, the hands from shivering, the sinews from shrinking, the veynes from crumplying, the bones from ayking, the marrow from soakying, and truly it is a sovereign liquor if it be orderlie taken."*

Imagine all that on the back label of a bottle of Chivas Regal or Talisker. Hmm. The lawyers would have a heyday. Safer to say Product of Scotland and define the category as per the Scotch Whisky Association's proposed definitions, which look set to be law by 2007:

- Single Malt Scotch Whisky
- Single Grain Scotch Whisky
- Blended (Malt and Grain)
- Blended Malt (Vatted)
- Blended Grain

What we each privately swear by is another matter. When asked what he believed the best cure for a cold to be, Sir Alexander Fleming, Scottish chemist and the discoverer of penicillin, answered, "A good gulp of whisky at bedtime – it's not very scientific, but it helps." In similar vein the late Doctor Dewar of St. Margaret's Hope, South Ronaldsay, Orkney, prescribed three fifths Highland Park and two fifths ginger wine as a restorative after "exposure to high gales and wild seas". So, eminent folk – indeed, pillars of society –

have kept faith with Holinshed down the centuries. I'm not sure about "kepyng the tongue from lispying" but a hot toddy of whisky, honey and lemon works wonders on a cold or sore throat, not least as it brings sweet oblivion speedily in its wake.

But if Holinshed spoke true on the virtues of Scotland's spirit he spoke false on the atrocities of two of Scotland's most famous people – the Macbeths. With the inestimable help of Shakespeare, for whom he acted as a prime source, he made these two infamous and synonymous with brutal, merciless ambition; the converse of alchemy – turning gold into base metal. Shakespeare, with a weather-eye on the new King Jamie's fascination, wove witchcraft into the mix too, painting Scotland as a barbaric wasteland. The reign of Macbeth and his consort Gruoch in fact accounted for 17 years of unbroken peace: something of a record. So the Holinshed/Shakespeare tale was probably one of the first myth makings that Scotland has been subject to. It is certainly one of the most famous and certainly not the last. As we shall see, Scotland is a nation much put upon by myth. This has direct bearing on the history of the branding of Scotch Whisky and, most significantly, the future possibilities. More of that later too.

Back to the sixteenth century. For around a hundred years, "uisge beatha" was a winter by-product of the farms, when the surplus grain from the harvest was distilled to make the fiery spirit so welcome on a cold northern night and, in time, seen as the perfect accompaniment to stories by the fireside, itself a mainstay of Celtic culture. The "water of life" and the secret of its creation, having passed from the spiritual realm to the temporal, and into the ken of courtier and commoner alike, wasn't for long going to conceal its commercial possibilities. John Haig & Co. claim to be the oldest distillers in the world – established by Robert Haig in 1627 in the Scottish Lowlands. By the 1670s there is the first mention of a distillery – Ferintosh – and by the 1760s, the poetic "uisge beatha" had been shortened to "uisky" and then whisky: shortened, one can only imagine, through a mix of affectionate familiarity and raw, eighteenth century marketing opportunism.

1. A well-known Edinburgh advertising agency is called 1576 after the date on the lintel of the first premises it occupied off The Royal Mile. The Glen of Tranquillity commercials for Glenmorangie, with the two guys on sofas in the middle of nowhere, are its creations.

2. A boll is six bushels. A bushel is eight gallons. So eight bolls is 544 gallons. A firlot, if you've ever wondered, is quarter of a boll. In other words, about 12 gallons. I just love the terminology. I wish we got our petrol in bushels and firlots. Bolls would be for pantechnicons. That was the kind of amount of malt Friar John Cor was getting signed off. He wasn't making cough mixture for a winter of sick brothers.

3. For the full set of "rare" tales visit *www.henzteeth.com*

4. "On the stair head … a drunken old hag in a greasy mutch (cloth cap) with trembling hands pours out from her black bottle a compound of whisky and methylated spirits, a glass of which being off in the dark and money paid, the recipient staggers down the stairs and out again to the streets." From Elspeth King's *Popular Culture in Glasgow*. Note that the whisky is mixed with methylated spirits. Before 1845, when the tax on glass was lifted, whisky was often adulterated with everything from tartaric to glycerine. In fact, it was when manufacturers, freed from the burden of the glass tax, started bottling and labelling their whisky that two things came into being: quality control and the beginning of branding. The industry today fiercely protects the quality of its products and has done since 1909, when the first all-important definitions were laid down in law. The word Scotch is an assurance of quality and the old mutched hag is a character more at home in today's ubiquitous ghost tours than the altogether more refined distillery tours.

5. Often mistaken to mean a disease due to strangling or choking. It is, in fact, a disease of the urinary organs characterised by slow and painful emission of urine.

CHAPTER 5
c.1823
FOUNDATIONS

Hergé, Belgian creator of Captain Haddock often drew a little white Haddock-faced angel on the captain's left shoulder and a little red Haddock-faced devil on his right. The advocates of sin and sanctity traded reason and emotion for the captain's will. The devil Haddock (smoked no doubt) often had a bottle of whisky in his hand. Interestingly, I can't remember what props the Haddock-faced angel employed. A twenty-first century Bowdlerizer might cleverly give the full-sized Haddock-faced man a shot glass and win the argument hands down with the wisdom of the middle path.

The virtue and vice debate around whisky has raged for centuries. In 1736, an early use of the word whisky appears in the Letter Book of Bailie John Steuart of Inverness – a cautionary letter to his brother-in-law asking him to "forbear drinking that poisonous drink, I mean drams of brandie and whisky; for certainly your lait maladie has been fostered that way ..." However, the same year, a traveller to Scotland wrote: "the ruddy complexion, nimbleness of these people is not owing to the water drinking but to that which is commonly used both as a victual and drink: Aqua Vitae, a malt spirit."

Enter the question of legality. In 1777, H. Arnott's *The History of Edinburgh* quoted an estimate of over 400 illegally operating stills in that city, as compared with eight licensed distilleries. In 1781, private distilling for home consumption was made illegal. What had become an inviolable right of every Scots man and woman, whether farmer, chemist, barber, butcher, baker or candlestick maker, was now denied. Certainly, there was the question of adulteration as touched on in a footnote in the previous chapter. And equally there were social problems caused by the availability of cheap strong liquor. But let's cut to the chase – here was a source of good brass, so much of it in fact that it had the glint of gold. And there were expensive wars against Old Boney and the French to pay for. Whisky was seen as a money-maker and the Treasury has been on its case ever since.

Commerce is the prey of government and to a degree rightly so. But there are many in the whisky industry, both today and in centuries past, who have felt that the degree of excise levied on whisky has always been unjustly high, and, for about 40 years, from the 1780s until the 1820s, the level of government interference, constraint and excise was such that many distillers operated outside the law, giving rise to a long period of smuggling and violent run-ins with the excise men[1] – a period sometimes referred to as "the whisky wars". The legal distilleries didn't benefit much either, being constantly undercut by the black market.

A favourite distillery of mine – Highland Park on Orkney – was founded by a smuggler in 1798.[2] I say a smuggler but that's only half the truth for Magnus Eunson was also a preacher: preacher by day, illicit distiller by night. The story goes that Eunson had his stills in a bothy, or shepherd's shelter, on the High Park. Not only was it well positioned for fresh water and a ready supply of peat but it also provided a good vantage point to watch out for the excise men. The bothy doubled as a meeting house or chapel, as was often the case in remote parts, and had a rough makeshift pulpit. It was under this pulpit that Eunson stashed the illegal apparatus when the call went up that the excise men were heading out from nearby Kirkwall, the island's capital. Eunson's moonshine cronies quickly took up their congregational stance whilst he, donning a shabby surplice no doubt, went into full flight about the depravity of the Israelites, swarthy heads turned by Ba'al, ecstatic, semi-clad dancing and prostrations before the venereal golden calf.

Some versions of the story have phlegmatic islanders hauling out a coffin complete with corpse and placing it over the stills and in front of the minister to receive last rites. There would be echoes here of their Viking ancestors hauling their long ships onto the sands at Ophir on the huge bay of Scapa Flow: the breaking of rules being coded in a deep vein. It was certainly a theatrical bothy, though this is probably a few planks too far: the Orcadians love a story. What is more than likely is that Eunson was the front man for a cartel of local businessmen, dignitaries and servicemen – the Orkney "mafia". When the distillery became legal in 1826 the site, which had already become known as Highland Park, quickly went into full operation. So there must have been solid investment already behind it. But whisky is a product that thrives on anecdote, apocryphal stories and romance. Embedded in its colourful history and diverse, singular, locations have always existed powerful elements of brand building that other brands would kill or sell subsidiaries or relatives for.

In the early 1820s, with the build up of pressure from just such cartels as in Orkney, the Duke of Gordon rallied the House of Lords to confront the chaotic state of affairs. And sense prevailed with the Excise Act of 1823: duty was cut dramatically and production and trading constraints were lifted. In effect, this was the beginning of the whisky industry in Scotland – with the support rather than the opposition of government. Many of the great distilleries were founded or became legal entities. The Glenlivet distillery was the first to take out a licence in 1824 under the new Act, followed by Cardhu and then The Macallan.

Another early licensed distillery was Glendronach near Huntly in Aberdeenshire. Licensed in 1826, it was built by James Allardice, the son of a local landowner, who knew the above-mentioned Duke of Gordon. Indeed the Duke was rather fond of this particular tipple so it might have had something to do with him "getting the Act together". Founders' stories are the bedrock of many a brand. Scotch Whisky has more than its fair share. Allardice's story, in its own way, is as colourful as Eunson's. Allardice was something of a pioneer in wood finishing, a preserve that's associated more these days with Balvenie, Glenmorangie and Bowmore, and a topic this narrative will touch upon again, but it's his entrepreneurial flair that helps bring the copy on the back label alive:

DISTILLED, MATURED AND
BOTTLED BY THE PROPRIETORS

The
GLENDRONACH DISTILLERY
C°LIMITED
LICENSED SINCE 1826
FORGUE BY HUNTLY
ABERDEENSHIRE
SCOTLAND AB5 6DB

THE 'GUID' GLENDRONACH

We know Allardice was on to a good thing. And so did he! Indeed he called his malt (in his Aberdeenshire brogue) 'The Guid Glendronach' and the first people he convinced of this were the ladies of the night who haunted Edinburgh's Canongate. Breaking into the market was proving difficult for Glendronach in 1826, so Allardice took matters into his own hands, shipped a barrel to Edinburgh and went out himself to canvass every outlet in the city he could find.

But everyone w
a hand and Alla
it for all its wo
his hotel he wa
who asked him
dram?" he excl
so he did. And t
how 'guid' the
was demandin
we've never lo

A brand that has certainly never looked back since its first whisky ran from its stills on Christmas Day 1887 is Glenfiddich. Glenfiddich's founder was William Grant, a tenacious man if ever there was. Son of a Dufftown tailor he served an apprenticeship as a cobbler, a trade maybe inspired by his grandfather who famously walked home to Scotland on being demobbed after the Battle of Waterloo in 1815. He must have worn out a

ABERDEENSHIRE
SCOTLAND AB5 6DB

JID' GLENDRONACH

g. And
in his
onach'
were
urgh's
was
6, so
ipped
elf to
find.

But everyone was stocked up. Then fate dealt
a hand and Allardice was canny enough to play
it for all its worth. Returning downhearted to
his hotel he was accosted by two young women
who asked him to buy them a dram. "Buy ye a
dram?" he exclaimed, "I'll gie ye a dram." And
so he did. And they liked it. And told their friends
how 'guid' the Glendronach was. Soon everyone
was demanding 'The Guid Glendronach'. And
we've never looked back since.

pair or two of shoes. The soldier, who lived on
this tale (I was going to say feat) for many a
year, depicted sturdy in kilt and tammy and
smoking a cob pipe, graciously accepted the
nickname Old Waterloo. What he had shown
were resolve and fortitude. Qualities that were
genetically transmitted. And continue to be so.

William Grant certainly possessed them. He
quickly moved on from leather to barley, an

element that held more promise. He worked for 20 years at the Mortlach Distillery, on £200 a year, learning every aspect of whisky production. During this time, he married and had seven sons and two daughters. And all the while, with 11 mouths to feed on a modest salary, he put money aside to fund his dream: "to create the best dram in the valley". The valley being the valley of the Spey – the heartland of Scotch Whisky. His wife, Anne, cannot be overlooked in the supreme effort the family made to realise this dream. What she must have gone without (furs, rubies and trips to Scarborough). The story goes that they were given a sixpence as a wedding gift. The phrase "And what they did with that sixpence ...!" has slipped into local folklore.

Grant's story demonstrates the sterling qualities that epitomise the Victorian age and the phenomenal commercial prowess that made a small country a great country. It's sometimes hard in post-colonial Britain (and Scotland at this time was referred to as North Britain) to take such stories square on without any side or sneer. Maybe it's a profound envy. But enough psychologising, we've left William and Anne in the midst of doing Highland alchemy with their sixpence. Once Grant had saved up £120 he bought a secondhand pair of stills from Cardhu Distillery for £119.19s.10d and with tuppence change in his pocket (enough for a couple of celebratory drams) he carted them over the hill to his chosen spot by the River Fiddich, which he'd bought from one of his other pots of savings. Like my canny Scots mother's brown teapot in which she saved up loose change I imagine one teapot in William and Anne's cottage saying Land and another saying Stills. And maybe there was a third, smaller teapot saying Stonemason, for once they'd got their land and their stills the whole family – parents, sons and daughters – built the distillery with their own bare hands with no outside help except for that of a stonemason.

Glenfiddich, along with Balvenie and William Grant's (one of the world's top-selling blends) has remained in the family for five generations. In the 1960s, the directors made the bold decision to market it as a single malt, introducing the world at large to the pleasures of unblended Scotch. The strategy worked: today, Glenfiddich is the world's best-selling single malt.

In the days before the patent still and the art of blending, there had been nothing but malts. But for over 100 years, blends, as we shall see, came to dominate the whisky scene and conquer the world; the Grant family played a big part in that too.

It was another enterprising Scot, Andrew Usher, who first successfully vatted a number of malt whiskies in 1853, which paved the way for blending. The idea of blending may have been borrowed from the tea merchants, who had started combining different leaves to make the perfect cuppa whether it were for the brickie or the English lady on her lawn. And I'm going to borrow from that dynamo of a whisky writer, Charles MacLean, to give a brief introduction to blending.

In his invaluable *vade mecum*, the Mitchell Beazley *Pocket Guide to Scotch Whisky*, MacLean quotes David Macdonald, former chairman of Macdonald Martin Distillers, who defined blending succinctly as, "The art of combining meticulously selected, mature, high quality whiskies, each with its own flavour and characteristics, with such skill that the whole is better than the sum of its parts, so that each makes its own contribution to the finished blend without any one predominating."

As MacLean explains, when the selected whiskies are all malts the result is called a vatted malt rather than a blend. Blended whisky is a mix of malt and grain whiskies and today this style of Scotch accounts for the overwhelming majority of sales worldwide. Typically, a blend will comprise between 15 and 40 different malt whiskies and two to three grains. The proportion of malt to grain is between 20 per cent and 60 per cent. Crucially, the so-called patent stills, which are used for blends, are completely different from the pot stills used for malt whisky. The patent still was perfected by an Irishman, Aeneas Coffey, in 1831 and its key feature was that it enabled continuous production.

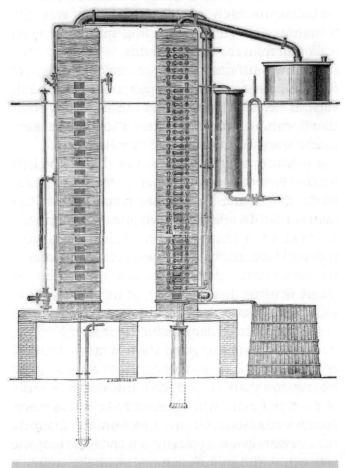

DRAWING OF THE COFFEY STILL

(Ironically, it was the Scots and not the Irish who were to benefit the most from this, as we will see below.) Today, Scotland's seven operating grain distilleries, which use the patent still with its two interconnected copper-lined columns, together have the capacity to produce 333 million LPA (litres of pure alcohol) per annum. A veritable Ganges of booze! Interestingly, not all of this output goes into blended whisky; much of the base spirit for gin and vodka comes from the same stills.

Malt whisky production is a batch process, and the equipment must be scrupulously cleaned after each round of distilling. Patent stills, on the other hand, can be run continuously for seven days before they require cleaning. The key benefit for the manufacturer is volume. But the key benefit for the consumer is consistency. Consistency was to be the key to massive popular appeal. Usher, like many of his distilling counterparts, was to make a fortune; a not immoderate chunk of which went into building Edinburgh's premiere concert venue, the Usher Hall. Listening to the pure strains of Nanci Griffith there recently, it was satisfying to muse on the rewards of consistency.

When I visited Glenmorangie's master blender, Rachel Barrie, in July 2005, she told me that the art of blending is like putting together a 1,000 piece jigsaw to create a perfectly integrated whisky flavour. It's here that the sensory skills face their greatest challenge. Rachel had discovered during the course of her organic chemistry degree that she was extraordinarily responsive to smell. Complex whiskies have over 20 aromas – Glenmorangie 10

Years Old, for instance, has 26 – and whereas Rachel can identify just about all these aromas, a novice could maybe identify between three and five (they might "get" vanilla, fruit and spice). About ten per cent of the population has this ability, and Rachel now tests for Glenmorangie's tasting panel. A test I'd love to undergo, and although I don't for a moment think I was born with such a nose, Rachel assured me one could tune and calibrate the olfactory sense. Inadvertently, as a student, she had hit upon the art to accompany her science that was to land her a job, aged 22, at the Scotch Whisky Research Institute and from there to Glenmorangie and up a tree usually only scaled by men. For Rachel, intuition and instinct were key attributes to her success. The chemistry is a tool to explain what's going on in the mystery; a mystery at the heart and soul of which is Mother Nature and Time. How refreshing it was to hear a scientist talk like this! Without playing down the science, though: she told me that whisky is a complete dream for the analytical mind.

Amongst her successes is the perfection of the Bailie Nichol Jarvie blend which has one of the highest malt profiles at 60 per cent and is a multi-award winner. Here, she has looked for very diverse malts and different grains, selecting complementary flavours to weave together an overall smooth whisky flavour. She doesn't work alone. She has a team. But her fellow traveller is Bill Lumsden, master distiller, and she described the joy of joint detective working, tracing back aromas and of being really specific in the final

BAILLIE NICHOL JARVIE

description, like lemon meringue pie (not lemony) or Toblerone (not nutty chocolate). "God is in the detail," she said. "And there's a real connection when you find something together." I could imagine. If only I hadn't found chemistry so dull and gassy at school. I sniffed and, being reminded of my blocked nose, I asked her if she was still able to recognise and describe an aroma with a cold. "Yes," she said, "The overall intensity is reduced but just blow your nose." Hay Fever, however, might affect the trigeminal nerves. And I couldn't overlook the fact she was pregnant; her third child. Had this affected her sensitivity? "Early on, the nasties were a lot more evident," she said. "There's a heightened sensitivity linked to the basic instinct of protecting the unborn child." And her other baby, the award-winning BNJ blend, would she divulge the recipe I asked, hoping against hope? A secret, she smiled.

Back 140 years … the patent still no longer an inventor's secret, The Spirits Act of 1860 allowed the blending of grain and malt whiskies from different distilleries for the first time. The scene was set for something big. Here was an industry suddenly ready to take off. New markets, especially in the British colonies were thirsty for it, finding whisky diluted with soda the perfect sun-downer in the heat of the tropics. But the final catalyst that propelled whisky into another league altogether was something very small: an insect. An insect that had come all the way from America to Europe. From the 1860s to the 1890s, the vineyards of France were ravaged by a virulent aphid called the *phylloxera vastatrix* ("the devastator"). This was disastrous for the grape crops. Disastrous, therefore, for brandy. And by the mid 1880s brandy – the preferred spirit of the English gentleman – was almost unavailable.

For whisky, this was a godsend no-one could have foreseen. And it was Scotch Whisky that took the greatest advantage of the situation, leaving the Irish competition trailing. Scotch filled the brandy vacuum. The Scots, in the form of remarkable entrepreneurs like Tommy Dewar and James Buchanan, took first London and then the Empire by storm with inspired marketing and salesmanship. In the art of raising profile, their stories are legend, and it was of their ilk that

DEWAR'S 'FOREFATHERS' ADVERTISEMENT – THE LONDON ILLUSTRATED NEWS 1897

J. M. Barrie,[3] the Scots author of Peter Pan, living in London at the time, said: "There are few more impressive sights in the world than a Scotsman on the make." Johnnie Walker's "Regency Buck" was created at this time. One of the earliest brand logos, it has become one of the most recognised logos ever. Later, following the installation of a giant whisky drinking Scotsman on the banks of the River Thames, Dewar's Whisky was the first product to be advertised on television.

Name	The Whisky of His Forefathers.
Designation	R.E.C. Taylor, Dan Ferguson and
Date Taken	Fraser, Commissionaire.

ACTORS FROM THE FIRST EVER CINEMA COMMERCIAL – DEWAR'S 'FOREFATHERS'

James Buchanan advertised both his and his whisky's presence in London by riding around in a red, emblazoned horse-drawn carriage. A tall thin man, impeccably presented and bearing a slight resemblance to Groucho Marx, Buchanan once pulled off a famous stunt by going to a restaurant that didn't stock his brand, with a rumbustious group of dashing beaux. They sat down at table and when asked for what aperitif they'd like, they answered in unison, "A Buchanan's". The poor waiter had to inform the party that, unfortunately, they didn't have Buchanan's. "What!" said the group again in unison. And standing up, thereby drawing the attention of all the diners in the room, they exclaimed "No Buchanan's!" and left in mock high dudgeon. History doesn't recall whether the proprietor was rattled enough to put in an order instantly but word certainly got about town that here was a whisky with panache. Today's industry might be as innovative as it ever was – it certainly has the creative minds – but it lacks Buchanan's calibre of showman.

Scotch had been dealt a brilliant hand: the patent still, the *phylloxera vastatrix* and an unrivalled

LANDSEER'S 'MONARCH OF THE GLEN'

breed of dashing entrepreneurs. But that was not the extent of its luck. Someone loved Scotland. Someone very influential. In fact, probably the most powerful person in the world at the time: Queen Victoria. She and Prince Albert fell in love with the romance of the Highlands, decking out their palatial country retreat, Balmoral, in tartan. Sir Walter Scott had introduced tartan into the royal wardrobe in 1822 when he hosted the famous visit of George IV to Edinburgh and had master-minded an Olympian-style display of Highlandism. Victoria would have met Scott when still a girl and had, no doubt, been enthralled by the stories of his homeland cast in myth and mystery. The majestic landscape did the rest, and she fully bought into the lifestyle of the Scottish aristocracy. She even commissioned the creator of *The Monarch of the Glen* (that painting of the stag against a dramatic slate-grey sky), Edward Landseer, to paint a huntin', shootin' and fishin' Highland Idyll with Queen and Consort as centrepieces, tartan-clad ghillies in attendance and the dead prey of river and air all around in a cornucopia of promised succulence.

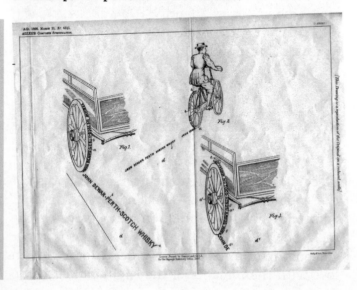

INNOVATIVE DEWAR'S ADVERTISEMENT PATENT APPLICATION
1897

The advance in rail travel at the same time meant that the English aristocracy who were getting a taste for good blended Scotch could also reach the Highlands much quicker than before and so share in this outdoors idyll. Victoria's influence, of course, spread far beyond the court and the ruling classes. Her age was the age of Empire and commerce and saw the real establishment of the merchant middle class. Virtually everyone was pulling in the same direction for their mutual benefit. So what the Queen favoured was favoured universally. And Victoria is largely responsible for the proliferation of the tartan and bagpipes imagery that still haunts Scotland and Scotch today. Still a very lucrative haunting for tourism and the perpetuation of clan affiliations – but arguably a millstone for post-devolution Scotland and twenty-first century Scotch in its striving for a new, contemporary identity. Nonetheless, back then, and for posterity, the Queen's love of Scotland turned this hand into a Royal Flush.

1. Famous Scottish excise men include poet Robert Burns, economist Adam. Smith and, more recently, writer Neil Gunn. Burns and Gunn both wrote memorably and passionately about whisky and saw it as a great egalitarian spirit – a sentiment that sometimes seems at odds with the luxury categories many brands espouse. But, as I said earlier, there are many worlds of whisky. And they are all connected, like a Venn diagram.

2. Interestingly, the first Bourbon whiskey was distilled in Bourbon County, Kentucky in 1789 by a Baptist minister: the Revd Elijah Craig. Another spirited Scot.

3. Johnny Depp, who played Barrie in the film *Neverland*, is on record as having a penchant for Lagavulin. He doesn't drink it anymore, his spirit drinking days being over, his palate being seduced by the softer joys of the grape. But he still likes to nose it, inhale its bouquet, savour the waft of peat, the hints of smoke and brine. Like perfume.

CHAPTER 6
∽1 THE ANGELS' SHARE

In Coigach the angels were waiting. There were the usual suspects. Gabriel with his necklace and locket bearing a photograph of Louis Armstrong. Michael dressed to the nines in dragon hide. And Raphael looking at the huge expanse of sky as if it were a canvas. They needed a place like Coigach to meet. They could each settle on a mountain (Suilven, Stac Pollaidh, Canisp, in neighbouring Assynt) like a mortal might settle on a sofa or an armchair. They were mighty entities. And when wingspan was taken into account they needed a bit of personal space. No place better than the majestic, mountainous West Coast overlooking the Atlantic and the Hebrides. They alternated between cloud cover and celestial camouflage to remain invisible to prying eyes.

The place was right geographically too. The angels – strictly speaking archangels – seldom all hooked up at once. And when they did it tended to be Scotland. And it tended to be here for the said geological reasons. But also, of course, though there are no distilleries in the immediate proximity, when there was a good, strong easterly blowing in from Siberia they got an excellent draught of their eponymous share. The first onslaught of evaporations might come from Glen Ord, Glen Albyn, and Glen Mhor; a second wave bringing the joys of Teaninich, Tomatin, Glenburgie and the spoils of Speyside in its current. Or a northerly swerve to the winds might bring in drifts of Dalmore, Glenmorangie and Balblair; a particularly strong blast catching wafts of Clynelish and Pulteney from further up the East

JOHN ALLERT AND PATRICK BERGEL'S ALCHEMICALLY INSPIRED LABEL FOR 26 MALTS

Coast. The landmass of Scotland is well served by the winds. Sooner or later, a spell in Coigach, chewing the divine cud and swapping tales of derring-do in the realms of the human psyche, would be accompanied by a fair share, the angels' share,[1] of just about every whisky in the land.

This share had been decreed a bonus for nigh on two hundred years. "You've never had it so good," was a phrase the Good Lord overheard in the 1950s and rather liked, and rather wished he'd overheard a lot sooner as it was a good political slogan that the angels couldn't immediately refute. I don't mean to presume in any way to know the mind of God, so I'll take you back to the angels. They were excited. The thing is their share had been getting better, richer, more varied as the years went by. There had always been a wonderful spectrum of taste and aroma to delight in: grass, hay, caramel, cinnamon, toffee, wood-smoke, lemon, autumn berries. For years, of course, there had been the tinges of vanilla and strains of the rye of bourbon and, in some up currents, the silky richness of sherry. But then strains of other wines started to appear, like port and madeira, and behind that, and behind the bourbon and sherried oak, a deeper, sweeter density of flavour. The angels were intrigued. Usually their interventions in human affairs were to do with matters of life and death. Gabriel, in particular, had something to blow his trumpet about on that count. Which he did from time to time when a westerly brought a pure draught of Talisker to his nostrils. In a sense, their interest here was to do with conception. And they had briefed one of their company, Azrael, to go down to the plains and valleys and find out what was occurring.

Now Azrael is the angel of death. He has feelers out everywhere. And he's a big fellow. The millennium edition of Brewer's *Phrase and Fable*, revised by Adrian Room, describes him thus: "He has four faces and four thousand wings and his whole body consists of eyes and tongues, the number of which corresponds to the number of people inhabiting the earth." So, there's a lot of Azrael. You'd notice him striding down any high street, let alone pitching up at the post office counter of a highland village asking for the way to the distillery. But he can transform. Of course he can. After all, Gabriel did. *He* was the original tall dark stranger. Two millennia later he'd have played sax and left before daylight. So, at the click of a finger, the crack of a knuckle, the crick of the neck, the slouch of a wing, Azrael scaled right down to the size of a man. He wore a soft moleskin coloured suit and the crispest white shirt this side of Hollywood. (Hollywood would love him actually, special effects would have a ball.) His tie was black and made of rough Asian silk. His shoes were Portuguese. He decided that handsome and charming were the best ways to present himself. And so attired and composed he set off.

Israfel, the angel commissioned to blow the trumpet of resurrection, was the first to spot the car. A dark horse musically, he was an excitable and chatty type. So at first, when he was pointing and circling his Concorde-like wings from the top of Ben Cogaich, the others didn't pay much attention. "That's Israfel'" they concurred, "practising semaphore." Of course the endgame angel couldn't squawk his horn for fear of rattling all that calcium. So he had to shout. And shout he did: "It's Azrael! In the black Chrysler." And he pointed way over Loch Broom to the road that wound up from Gairloch past Inverewe Gardens and the radiation-free Gruinard to a shining Chrysler Cruiser heading ineluctably towards the mighty mountain of An Teallach ("the anvil" in Gaelic and pronounced "an challach", like a chalice of hard stones). All the angels kept their sights focused on the stylish retro-car that looked like it could have driven out of a 30s gangster movie. It could have been a bootlegger's in Prohibition USA. For sure, the angel in this car carried a message about whisky.

At the foothills of An Teallach, Azrael stopped the car and got out. There wasn't a speck of dust on him. On a clear night – that when it shows, shows brilliant in these parts – you could see the stars reflected in the polish of his shoes. But this was broad daylight. And if anyone in the vicinity, deer stalker, creel hauler, ferry man, had seen what happened next they would either have blotted it out or gone to see a shrink. Unknotting his tie and letting it trail behind him, almost thoughtlessly, like a horse whisperer's lead rope, he started to stride uphill through the whin and the heather. Then a serpentine flame shot up the black silk as if from the earth and set his suit alight. The angel of death simply stepped out of the blaze, bigger by half, his shoulders branching into wings. With each stride he grew again, making his ascent of An Teallach look like stepping up a ladder to change a bulb. On the top he gathered himself to his full height and width and sat like a squat and massive Buddha in an unassailable lotus.

"Wood," he boomed across the loch to the other enthroned angels at a frequency only a nervy hound could pick up. "They've gone into the heart of wood and found its magic there."

TREE SLICE OF OZARK OAK

"Wood," murmured the others.

"Oak?" bellowed Michael.

"Of course," replied Azrael.

"And three years' minimum ...?"

"Yes, yes," came the testy reply. "The statutory requirements hold. Scotch Whisky has to be matured for a minimum of three years in oak barrels or casks in Scotland. Hurrah!"

"Hurrah!" echoed the others.

"Of course, it wasn't always thus," said Gabriel. "Once upon a time farmers would leave it to mature in any container, wood or otherwise, though mostly wood, or stone ..."

"You've got a long memory Gabriel," said Raphael.

"And a largely irrelevant one too," snapped Azrael, who was keen to get on with his report. He asked them to conjure up in their minds all the bonded warehouses tucked away in highland glens, or on the outskirts of cities like Glasgow and Edinburgh, or perched above island shorelines. He asked them to look inside and see the countless thousand racks of barrels, sometimes the height of three men and requiring a forklift to bring them down.

"Oak casks," he purred, "holding God knows how many zillion litres of maturing whisky."

"I prefer bolls myself," said Michael.

"Steady on with the minor blasphemies Mike."

"For centuries, batch loads of whisky have lain for 8, 10, 12, 15, 18 or more years in wood, oak wood ..."

Gabriel raised his finger but Azrael ignored him.

"... not resting or sleeping as some of the earthly scribes have been wont to describe the whisky's incumbency ..."

"Once he gets going he's really quite eloquent," said Gabriel to Israfel, who was lapping it all up and just nodded silently.

"... but reacting with the wood chemically."

"Mirroring the maturation of mortals!" exclaimed Raphael.

"Yes, of course," said Azrael. "Mellowness comes by way of hard knocks, by learning give and take."

"There's fire in whisky's mellowness."

"And depths."

"Which is why we angels savour it so much," said Raphael. "It gives us a glimpse of the noble but hard-won spirit of man."

The angels were getting quite animated now, jostling about in a kind of juggernaut dance on their respective mountain tops.

"But it's only recently that they've discovered the extent of the activity in the barrel and the huge influence wood has on the whisky," said Azrael.

BILL LUMSDEN CHECKING THE QUALITY OF OAK

And he proceeded to tell the others what he had learnt in his sojourn in Scotland visiting distilleries, talking to "noses", calling in at cooperages, stopping over at homely B&Bs, sleeping under tartan-covered duvets and once, just once, experiencing a proper high tea.[2]

He told them how certain master distillers and industry chemists had started to analyse and better understand the internal structure of wood. It had to be oak, but there are different types of oak – Spanish, Limousin, Missouri. He told them how these species grow at different rates, which in turn determines whether a wood has a tight or spaced grain structure. He explained how this structure affects porosity and the degree to which the whisky soaks into the barrel. He spoke of the experiments in air seasoning to break down lignin and tannin polymers; the dry kilning of staves, the heavy or "alligator" charring of the insides of casks; the subtleties of toasting via infra-red heat; the art on deciding on first fill; the oxidisation effects of finishing in sherry butts or port pipes, madeira drums or bourbon barrels. He painted a broad picture of an amazing creativity within set parameters (parameters laid down in law[3]) the end result of which was greater texture and sweetness and flavour.

"Whisky," he concluded, "just gets better." This was merely confirmation of all that the angels had been noting as the customary evaporation from the warehouses of Scottish distilleries came their way as if by divine grace. The sun was beginning to set on the mountains and over the sea. Looking up at the rock faces glinting in mellow gold you could almost imagine angels stopping there: to take in the view, to breathe in the air, to taste the spirit of this ravishing country. Maybe as you soften in this reverie you'd like to think the angels gentler beings than I've described, more like the androgynous harp-players of church windows. But no. I speak thus of the angels for whisky is a mighty spirit and invokes such guardians.

1. When the whisky is in cask, "resting" for a number of years in the warehouse, there's always a certain amount of evaporation. Go into any distillery warehouse and the smell is gorgeous. The proportion that is lost through evaporation has always been called "the angels' share". The girls in Chapter 1 debate about the place of the apostrophe. But being the right side of the pond we know. Of course it's angels plural.

2. High tea is a peculiarly Scottish combination of tea and supper – rare these days – where a hot dish like fish and chips is accompanied by scones and cakes and a pot of tea. Excellent after a day's sailing or hill walking.

3. By 1915, for any spirit to be called Scotch Whisky it had become mandatory, not only that it was produced and matured in Scotland but that it had been matured, for at least three years, in oak barrels. No artificial additives are allowed in the production of Scotch Whisky. The Scotch Whisky Association holds rigorously to this stipulation, enshrined in law, as it is an amazing guarantee of provenance, quality and purity. As a brand it is inviolable. All the more reason to laud the innovations being made in areas like wood management. As any artist knows, the more the strictures the greater the creativity.

CHAPTER 7
1745–1823
THE CREATION
OF A MYTH

In 1822, one year before the Excise Act, two years before the first distillery – Glenlivet – was licensed and 23 years before Andrew Usher vatted his first malts, an extraordinary thing happened in Edinburgh. George IV made a royal visit: the first monarch to visit Scotland since James VI and I in 1607. And George a German (with a vein or two of Scots let's not forget)! After James's short and disgruntled visit the Stuart line, a Scottish line that ruled over the Union of the Crowns for over 100 years (with a little Proletarian and then a little Orange interlude) never set foot north of the border. They were turbulent years, of course, but by the time the fourth Hanoverian was on the throne of the United Kingdom religious sectarianism was far less volatile and there were no forthcoming pretenders to the crown.

GEORGE IV'S ROYAL VISIT TO HOLYROOD 1822

The visit was masterminded by the writer Sir Walter Scott, a novelist first and foremost but also a spin doctor extraordinaire. Scott wanted to celebrate Scottishness but within a Unionist context. He had expended much energy reviving old ballads from his native Borders and had written historical romances about many Scottish heroes from Rob Roy to Montrose. What he pulled off with George's visit was an extravagant extension of his revivalist concerns and one of the biggest marketing creations of all time. Essentially, he established the Highlands as the brand image of Scotland and, by encouraging the king to embrace everything Highland, to wear Highland dress and be received in a Highland-bedecked Edinburgh, Scott achieved the royal stamp of approval. This was the culmination of a movement that had been taking place since the defeat of Bonnie Prince Charlie at the Battle of Culloden in 1745.

The irony is that 75 years before this Highlanders were seen as rebels and, worse, as Papists – savage Papists at that. But just as the Christian church, centuries before, had skilfully incorporated pagan sites and customs into their places of worship and their calendars, so the political architects behind the Hanoverian supremacy cleverly incorporated the enemy energy and resource into the very fabric of not only Scotland's identity but also a militaristic icon of the burgeoning British Empire.

I am not an historian and much of what follows was culled from Tom Devine's fascinating chapter on Highlandism in *The Scottish Nation: 1700–2000*. Fascinating in this context because the historical phenomenon of Highlandism has largely forged the universal image of Scotland and, by default, whisky. Many of Scotland's contemporary image-makers, and not just those in the whisky industry, are fighting to throw off this legacy and at the same time seeking other more contemporary imagery with which to replace it. But it still has a stronghold on the popular imagination.

Many people in the world today, if asked, would say that Scotland is a highland country – a land of mountains and lochs with accompanying Highland icons of the kilt and the bagpipe and, of course, the all-pervasive national garb, the tartan. There are Scots who profit from this – those who own the tourist stores along Edinburgh's High Street for starters – but the notion is really quite bizarre. This image hardly reflects the truth, as Scottish society is one of the most urbanised in the world. By the late nineteenth century Scotland had become an industrial pioneer, with the vast majority of its people engaged in manufacturing and commercial activities and living in the central Lowlands. Most rural areas by that time were losing population rapidly through migration to the Lowland cities. The Lewis poet Iain Crichton Smith called Glasgow the "Highland City" because so many Highlanders had gone to live there, after the Highland Clearances, (when crofters were infamously driven off their tenanted land to make way for more profitable sheep). The lure was work in the emerging industries, particularly the shipyards along the River Clyde which were to earn Glasgow its better known title – Second City of the Empire. Yet, despite this it was the Highlands, the most underdeveloped and poorest of all the Scottish regions, that provided and still provides the main emblems of cultural identity for the country as a whole. As Devine puts it, "An urban society had adopted a rural face."

Stranger still, the Highlands were and remain the land of the Gaels, the culturally distinctive and linguistically separate descendants of the Celts. There was a deep cultural divide between the under-populated and Gaelic Highlands and the Scots Lowlands. In fact, the Gaelic word Sassenach was originally ascribed to the Lowland Scots and not the English. The contempt was a two-way affair as contempt inevitably is. So what was it that the Highlands had that was so precious? It's not hard to answer that question today. Few would disagree that the Highlands of Scotland is one of the most beautiful regions on the planet. God's country is a phrase that's often attributed to it. Other parts of the world might make this claim too, but not many, and it's thanks only to the unreliability of the weather and the indigenous demon midge that the place isn't strafed by highways, high-rise hotels and villas.

However, it was not always perceived thus. Partly it was an aspect of anti-Highland satire to view the Highlander as one who inhabited a world of desolation, barrenness and ugliness. In the *Gazette* of 1800 this un-enticing description appears: "the North division of the country is chiefly an assembly of vast dreary mountains". This perception was also culturally defined. Dr Johnson was repelled and astonished by "the wide extent of hopeless sterility" during his celebrated journey to the Western Isles in 1773. Heather-covered bens were neither romantic nor attractive (as they were later to become) but merely ugly and sinister. Romanticism and concepts of noble, savage and primeval beauty were to change that, and, of course, Sir Walter Scott was a leading proponent of romantic writing. Scott helped popularise places like Loch Katrine and – for the ultimate encounter with the sublime wild – the Hebrides. Modern notions of scenic beauty were born at this time – much of them deriving from German philosophers and German artists such as Mendelssohn. Links with Germany were intellectually and commercially deep-rooted and went far beyond the inter-relations of the monarchy.

Also, by the early nineteenth century an upper class tourist trade was already established, partly because European travelling was made more difficult during the French wars. At the same time, the study of geology and its great contribution to a scientific view of the world was helping to change perceptions of this rugged wilderness. Some of the world's oldest rock formations were to be found in the Highlands, and Scotland was to produce many pioneering geologists over the next century.

All of this is background to understanding the extraordinary political volte-face that took final effect in 1822. At the heart of the politics was religion. Bonnie Prince Charlie is seen as a romantic figure today and has been for almost two centuries. But that is a deliberately manufactured image. The threat of his uprising (he almost succeeded) cannot be underestimated. For the

EDOUART SILLOUETTE OF SIR WALTER SCOTT

greater populace, it wasn't an issue of the dynasty with the more legitimate right to the throne; it was a matter of which religion claimants espoused: Catholic or Protestant. Probably more blood has been shed in the name of the Christian God than any other. Bonnie Prince Charlie was a Catholic and as such was seen by many as the Antichrist. This perception accounted for much of the hysterical and brutal reactions to the rebellion. The Highlanders' support of the pretender's claim meant that they became immediately associated with popery, which, added to the perception that they were also a collection of savage tribes, turned them into considerable bogeymen. It's maybe difficult today to appreciate the magnitude of the threat Bonnie Prince Charlie posed. In his march on London, which was not repelled by force but put into reverse on account of dubious military advice, the Young Pretender got as far as Derby. In other words, closer to the jugular of England than even Napoleon or Hitler; only William of Normandy and Oliver Cromwell outstripped him. Accordingly, the aftermath of the Battle of Culloden was intensely bloody with atrocious reprisals being carried out the length and breadth of the Highlands. As part of this, the Disarming Act of 1746 disallowed clansmen not only to carry arms but also to wear their traditional garb. It was a case of severe cultural suppression.

Having crushed the rebellion, the nation of Scotland needed to be rebuilt and unified and brought once and for all into the fold of the United Kingdom. That was the view of those in power.

And that's what they did. The period when the Disarming Act was in force (1746 – 1781) was the time that tartan and plaid started to become popular among the Lowland upper and middle classes of Scotland. This strange development was part of a wider process through which mostly imagined and false Highland "traditions" were absorbed freely by the Lowland elites to form the symbolic basis of a new national identity. Highlandism, Devine contends, was quite literally the invention of a tradition. What made it deeply ironic was not simply the historic Lowland contempt for ancient Gaelic culture that existed well into the century but also the fact that Highlandism took off precisely at the same time that commercial landlordism, market pressures and clearances were destroying the old social order in northern Scotland. And this was not simply a case of English domination: it was largely fuelled by Highland proprietors who had long ceased to be clan chiefs.

During this time, in 1761, James Macpherson produced his alleged Celtic "epic" *Fingal*. Macpherson claimed that he had discovered and translated a manuscript from an untamed and rugged pre-Christian Golden Age, and that the original author was third-century bard Ossian. Literary critics are mostly of the opinion that he made the whole thing up. Whatever, it was a huge success. The Celtic Highlands and its myths were beginning to capture the popular imagination far and wide. Even Napoleon, who took a trunk of books on campaign with him was said to count *Fingal* amongst his favourite works.

The first production of *Macbeth* in 1773 saw the hero dressed in tartan, an innovation that quickly became established as a stage tradition. In 1778, the Highland Society was founded in London. And four years later when the Disarming Act was repealed, tartan was rehabilitated and became swiftly fashionable. In 1789, the year that Charles Edward Stuart, bonnie no longer, died an alcoholic wreck in Rome, three of King George III's sons, including the future king George IV, were provided with complete Highland dress. One can only guess the commission value of Allan Ramsay's poem 'Tartana', written to promote Scottish textiles.

Seldom throughout history has myth-making been at such a pitch. A vital piece of the political jigsaw, of course, was to romanticise the Jacobite cause now that the threat had been well and truly crushed. In song and portrait Bonnie Prince Charlie was systematically turned from warrior and statesman into lover and gallant. Bonnie Prince Charlie was re-branded. In an astoundingly short space of time as well. But it's a spirit of romanticism that has, for many, deep sentiment, fuelled maybe by the unfailing comfort of the impossible dream. For instance, at Traquair House in the Scottish Borders – the oldest continuously inhabited house in Scotland – the Jacobite Maxwell-Stewarts have ordained that the gates at the end of their green driveway – The Bear Gates – will not be opened until a Stuart monarch ascends the throne again. And four hundred miles away in Oxford, at my old college, Trinity, there was this same

Jacobite rusted seal upon the college's wrought-iron garden gates. The sentiment extends far beyond Scotland. And the fact that the power of that romance, of that impossible dream, can be felt by those who know nothing of the story or the allegiances it encodes is witnessed every time the 'Skye Boat Song'[1] is sung with feeling and pure voice. It speaks of what might have been – whatever the context – for all of us. It answers for a while, for a night-capped night and a heart-warmed walk in the starlight, an insatiable yearning.

The clansmen also went through a metamorphosis from faithless traitors to heroic warriors as they were corralled into military service. Following the French Revolution the new threat was no longer Catholicism but Republicanism, and the vaunted (although manifestly pragmatic) transfer of loyalty from the Stuarts to the Hanoverians enabled Jacobitism to be redefined as an ideology committed to monarchy at a time when the British institution was under attack from radical enemies both within and without. The reputation of the Highland regiments in the Napoleonic wars lent a new prestige and glamour to the wearing of tartan. But for a brilliant insight into the diehard prejudice against Highlanders read Canadian writer Alistair MacLeod's *No Great Mischief*. The title is taken from General Wolfe's remark about the expendability of the Highlanders in his army. Contemplating the challenge in front of his men in scaling the cliffs to take Quebec in 1759 he said that if amongst his men the Highlanders were to lose their step and fall it would be "no great mischief".

As I've already said, the apotheosis of this transformation came in 1822 with the remarkable celebration of the visit of George IV to Edinburgh, a two-week extravaganza with events based on Highland and Celtic themes stage-managed by Sir Walter Scott. A further irony here is that Edinburgh had always been the Lowland city. It was, after all, the city of John Knox, the father of Scottish Presbyterianism. It was also the city of the Scottish Enlightenment, which so affected Europe's notions of civilisation, the workings of human nature and monetary capital. When Bonnie Prince Charlie had taken Edinburgh in 1745, Edinburgh society had, quite naturally, hosted parties in his honour and clapped politely at the kilted cavalcade of Highlanders making their way down the Royal Mile. But they were pleased when his army headed south. And delighted when the threat to their comfortable existence was finally quashed at Culloden.

It's interesting that in the subsequent expansion of Edinburgh, the names of so many of the streets in its elegant New Town are Hanoverian – Hanover, George, Frederick, Princes (in honour of George III's three sons) – or Unionist as in Rose and Thistle streets. And there's even a Cumberland Street after "Butcher Cumberland" the Royal Hanoverian Duke who defeated Bonnie Prince Charlie at the Battle of Culloden then ordered reprisals in the Highlands. The original design for the New Town was based on the Union Jack. Edinburgh was saying where its sympathies lay in no uncertain terms: in stone and architecture. Not that the Jacobite view of the throne was anti-unionist but the Catholic dimension would have caused continued shockwaves and unrest. In contrast, the Hanoverian incumbency stood for stability, the main concern for the prospering merchant classes.

A further irony in this cascade of ironies was that George IV was a vain and deeply unpopular king. But his unpopularity was beside the point, and his reign was to prove a blip in the wider, imperial scheme of things. What is hard to appreciate maybe is the influence Sir Walter Scott enjoyed. Imagine J. K. Rowling inviting today's Queen to Edinburgh Castle and asking her to dress up as a witch, Professor McGonagall no less, to oversee a parade of elite wizards, witches and warlocks, with cheering muggle subjects beyond the esplanade where the Tattoo is normally held. Can't quite do it? No, neither can I. But Scott was pulling off just as great, if not a greater fiction. Only it was deeply endorsed politically and was, in essence, a very clever colonial coup. The enduring seal of approval, of course, was that of Queen Victoria and Prince Albert. But the coup had been pulled off by the time of Victoria's succession. The rebel spirit had been taken into the heart of national identity. And this national identity was soon to be an imperial identity in which Highland Tartan Scotland was to play a crucial, highly visible and lauded part – particularly in the armed forces.

This was the backdrop to the emergence of Scotch Whisky on to first the English and then the

colonial market. The manufacturers were in little doubt as to the efficacy of this powerful Scottish imagery. In fact, there was no real choice. To embrace Highlandism made pre-eminent commercial and marketing sense. But herein lies the paradox at the heart of the industry today. Whilst much of the world still sees Scotland through a tartan lens, and this image helps sell whisky it no longer fits comfortably with the UK population at large. To the younger generations, it's stuffy, dominant, unenlightened, even racist.

Post devolution, Scotland is a nation once again looking to redefine its identity. Fashion and music are two industries that have successfully combined tradition (tartan and folk tunes) with new global influences to reflect a new cosmopolitan Scottish mindset. Emerging industries like computer games, life sciences, extreme sports and the festival culture all bring new definitions to what modern Scotland is. This is a wonderful opportunity for the Scotch Whisky industry to revisit its imagery – a gauntlet some brands have taken up with relish. Others await the brand visionary.

1. Speed bonnie boat like a bird on the wing
   Onward the sailors cry
   Carry the lad that's born to be king
   Over the sea to Skye
   Loud the wind howls, loud the waves roar,
   Thunderclaps rend the air
   Baffled our foes, stand by the shore
   Follow they will not dare

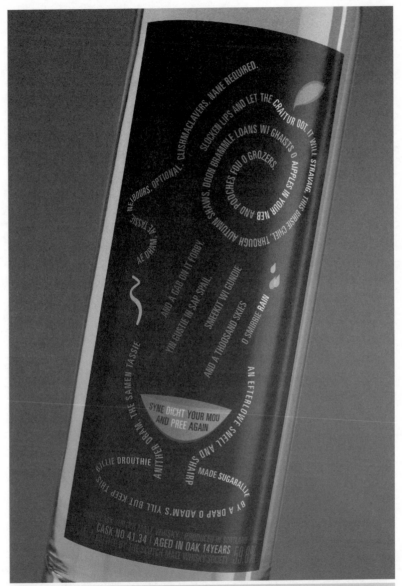

POET MATTHEW FITT HAD THIS TO SAY ABOUT HIS 26 LABEL WRITTEN IN SCOTS AND DESIGNED BY DAMIAN MULLAN: "DAMIAN AND I HOPE THAT OUR UNCO GALLUS LABEL WILL HAVE CONNOISSEURS BLETHERIN AND BLOUSTERIN AS THEY WEET THEIR GIZZEN WITH THIS BIRSIE CHIEL OF SPEYSIDE MALT."

CHAPTER 8
1995–2002
TELLING
STORIES

In July 1995, after three years running the Arvon Foundation's Devon centre at Totleigh Barton then a couple of years lecturing at several further education colleges in Edinburgh, I re-entered the world of commercial writing. (I came to live in Scotland as my wife, who is from the Scottish Borders, wanted to return home, after a seven-year sojourn south, to pursue a career in the theatre.) I say re-entered the world of commercial writing because from 1985 to 1990 I worked as an advertising copywriter in London and the south west of England. This itself had been a diversion from my "one true path" writing poetry and plays but even the old cliché "needs must" couldn't prevent me feeling I had sold out and was now a painted lady of the night-black ink. My re-entry into this world – again a case of "needs must" as neither the worlds of literary administration nor part-time lecturing provided sufficient to keep a young family in shoes and rusks – was to mark a gradual transformation of self-image, from "old tart" to "friendly chameleon". Much of this was down to moving from advertising to the more considered and serious world of design; and to writing about whisky.

At Redpath Design in Edinburgh, in a townhouse that used to serve as an undertaker's and only had one black telephone when we moved in, my chequered career finally started to bleed into parallel lines. The consultancy had recently been set up by Richard Irvine, a commercial writer who had been churning out annual reports very profitably during the fat Thatcher years. He wanted to do more exciting work than that which is often handed out to the freelance writer, to ensure that writing was more integral to the conceptual and creative process, and he hit upon the adventurous if not unique notion of setting up a consultancy where writers and designers worked in creative partnership very much as art directors and copywriters work in advertising. I was Richard's first mouse-manipulating guinea pig. (One of the first things I had to master was the personal computer, having been brought up on a typewriter and even having had the luxury of a secretary and a typing pool at my disposal. And it was a PC not a Mac; in the days when pcs were still strictly non-intuitive and, as Umberto Eco perceived, "Calvinist".)

Commercial writing in Scotland is fed largely from three sources: the financial sector, government agencies (including tourism and research) and the distilling industry. Yes, there's technology, utilities, science, construction, the professions and the arts but these are the big three. Whisky, without question, is the most glamorous of the three. It's a good product and an interesting one. There's a story to tell. The one I'm telling, in part and from a very personal point of view, here. The story involves people, craft, provenance and history. And the industry as a whole is open to a more artistic use of language, is more open to storytelling, is more open even – maybe unwittingly – to poetry, because at the end of the day this is a spirit that affects the senses – appearance, aroma and taste. Even sound: the whine and pop of the cork followed by the glugging pour of spirit into glass is for many as satisfying a sound as the litany of the shipping forecast. It heralds the prospect of unwinding and rejuvenation, relaxation and the sharing of anecdotes; and after another pop and pour the prospect of warmth in the blood and the pleasure of waxing lyrical.

So, great stuff to write about. Especially for a hedonist. And Redpath had a great client – Matthew Gloag & Son (which became Highland Distillers and is now the Edrington Group but I'm not going to even teeter around the threshold of buy-outs and the intricacies of ownership within the industry: that's the bread and butter of the business pages; great brands live on, whoever owns them – Scotsmen, Frenchmen or Japanese consortia). Brands in the Matthew Gloag portfolio included The Macallan, Highland Park, Bunnahabhain, The Glenrothes and Scotland's best selling blend The Famous Grouse. Great whiskies, great brands, although one of the first jobs I had at Redpath was to come up with a name for a new brand destined solely for the Indian market. The Indian market is a law unto itself and all the traditional Scottish imagery still has great purchase. I remember scribbling down hundreds of names from ploughing the regimental and militaristic furrow: amongst them were Big Meg (Edinburgh's famous One O'clock Gun), Highland Charge and The '45. Blue Blazer, extraordinarily, was the name that rang the marketing manager's bell.

Of course, The Famous Grouse in terms of its brand heritage epitomises so much of the colonial/Victorian history touched upon in previous chapters. It evokes the world of the hip flask on the moor, the attendant ghillie, shooting parties gathering in the rather faded and comfy grandeur of the "big hoose" or shooting lodge with stags' heads mounted on shields above fireplaces and lining heavy oaken and wide stairwells. And, of course, not only the English gentry and the new well-heeled classes still enjoy Scotland's big outdoors and subscribe to this image, but so do hordes of Americans and Germans and Japanese. But to be Scotland's No 1 Blend a whisky has to appeal to an audience far wider than this elect. There's aspiration, yes. Who in the world of marketing doesn't know about the perennial, seductive power of aspiration. But the truth is The Famous Grouse is a good dram. I had my first taste in the Jolly Judge pub off Edinburgh's Royal Mile 13 years earlier in 1982, accompanied by a pint of heavy (the way to wrack and ruin) when I was visiting the Fringe with my play *The Real Lady Macbeth*, debunking another great Scottish myth – that Macbeth was a good apple tempted and gone bad, topped up with poison by his ruthless lady wife. History reveals the converse. Their marriage unified the warring Picts and Scots and they reigned over 17 years of peace, unprecedented in those supposedly bloodier times. But we are jelly in the hands of the myth-makers, great story-tellers all. The Grouse itself was on the cusp of going through an advertising transformation:

going from the brightly plumed subject of a naturalist painting as might be seen hanging in a traditional highland lodge to a skittering cartoon bird that inhabited a blank canvas upon which he could be the fall guy to a series of witty twists on whisky terminology. There's a particularly good set of Grouse antics hanging on the walls of the gents' loo at West Kinfauns, the Edrington HQ.

One of the reasons The Famous Grouse is such a good dram is that it has at its heart a generous amount of Highland Park Single Malt Scotch Whisky. The drinks writer Michael Jackson (and not his pigment-scouring namesake) calls the classic Highland Park 12 Year Old "the greatest all-rounder in the world of malt whisky". And American whisky critic Paul Pacult also eulogises about this "utterly sensational malt" that "sings and zings on the palate". I spent six years – 1996 to 2002 – working with this brand (after which I left Redpath to set up my own company, Henzteeth, with fellow writer John Ormston). It's the brand I know best. In fact, I worked with three different brand managers during those years, Sarah Gilchrist, Tim Patterson and Nicole Walton, and by the time I was working with Nicole on the brand PR toolkit (complete with compass to denote the Northernmost Scotch Whisky Distillery in the World[1] and brand bible presented as a pack of playing cards[2]) I, not she, was definitely the repository of brand wisdom. However, she had great Aussie style and marketing nous plus a good feel for language. I remember an enjoyable half hour wrangling over whether to use the word heliocentric to describe Orkney's Neolithic culture on one of the "biblical" playing cards. She won. I wrote "Three of the key ceremonial sites attest to a sun-centred culture." Now whether she was right ...

Each of the brand managers at what by now was Highland Distillers was a joy to work with or alongside: they were all extremely bright, had a broad frame of reference and were passionate about their brands with an eye for detail that was spurred by the pursuit of excellence and not the

HIGHLAND PARK 18 YO. ILLUSTRATION OF THE RING OF BRODGAR BY ANDREW DAVIDSON

covering of their arses. Under Sarah Gilchrist's holding-of-the-reins, working in a team with designer Iain Lauder, we helped launch Highland Park 18 Year Old and 25 Year Old. One of the great strengths with the branding of malt whisky is provenance. United Distillers (once DCL now Diageo and tomorrow who knows and God forbid "The Whole Shebang"!?) had already caught on to the storytelling and positioning potential of regionality and had released their six classic malts – Glenkinchie, Oban, Talisker, Lagavulin, Dalwhinnie and Cragganmore – to great effect. In one fell swoop this allowed brands to disinvest themselves of the national trappings of myth and tartan and to break out of the colonial mould. One of the most successful brands to have achieved a

GREAT MALT, NO FRILLS PACKAGING. WORKS A TREAT.

"local" look and feel is Allied Distillers' Laphroaig. In its simple white tube with the little black ink illustration of a quayside bar, it comes across as totally local, totally unpretentious, no dressing. It is what it is. And it's strong, like a dredging sea wave with a spray of fire – peaty, smoky, briny. As the brilliant advertising campaign said – you either hate it or love it. There's no in-between. Go to Port Ellen where the salt winds have stripped the paint from hotel frontages and bitten into the wooden lintels and you'll see where the inspiration for that illustration hails from. It's a great brand. I'm a "friend". I have a plot of turf[3] on Islay: number 250549. At the home of Laphroaig. For there is, and can ever only be, one home: at Laphroaig.

This singularity of malt whisky is a tremendous strength when it comes to brand positioning and differentiation. It's at the opposite end of the spectrum from blended whisky, which takes a select range of malts and grains to make a smooth, consistent dram. Malts are rugged individuals, or more precisely, each distillery is like a family of rugged individuals with different age expressions, maybe different wood finishes, vintages, reserves, vattings – all bearing a family resemblance or house style but each distinct, lighter with youth, deeper, smoother, richer with age and the beneficence of time in the cask; a star gene at vintage.[4]

At my first meeting on the Highland Park account at West Kinfauns outside Perth, Iain Lauder and I met Sarah Gilchrist and marketing director Gerry O'Donnell. It was the only time I remember meeting Gerry. For me, his ha'pence still has the glint of gold. The standard Highland Park expression was a 12 year old. It came in a tube. And on the tube was a photographic motif of the midnight sun, a seasonal phenomenon of the northern latitude of the Orkneys along with the northern lights. How were we going to package the 18 and the 25 year olds? Gerry had already thought about this and talked about trading up in insights about Orkney as the consumer traded up in value with regards the malt. Connecting more fully with the brand would mean connecting more deeply with the brand's provenance, Orkney. The consumer would connect through stories. For the 18 Year Old we chose Orkney's Neolithic history. Orkney has in the region of 3,000 Neolithic sites (more are found every year by farmers ploughing up their land but are often quickly earthed up again to keep the antiquaries and ley hunters away) the most famous of which are Skara Brae, Maes Howe, the Tomb of the Eagles and the Ring of Brodgar. We chose the Ring of Brodgar to be the image for the 18 Year Old as standing stones are instantly recognisable. In retrospect, I like to think that we were also following the sun, for the headstones of the Ring are so positioned to catch the rays of the rising sun on midsummer morning (around 2.15 am – it's a good post-party expedition). But I think that came later, after we began to immerse ourselves in this extraordinary archipelago with its distinct culture, midway between Scandinavian and Scots.

Orkney was a Danish dominion until the middle of the fifteenth century. So the Orcadians have more than their fair share of Viking blood and are steeped in the Norse culture of sagas and heightened storytelling. This was the insight we wanted to convey in the packaging copy of the 25

Year Old. This expression retailed at £99 (it's more now) so the packaging had to be a little special. It was a wooden tube with a swing hinge door and bijou latch. And the copy was presented in flowing calligraphy on the inside panel of the door. It read:

Since the days of the heroic Norse Sagas, Orkney has inspired the spirit of the storyteller. As, since 1798, has Highland Park with its lovingly crafted mellowness.

Forever I flush the winters of men with wassails of corn

From 'John Barleycorn' by George Mackay Brown

In a culture whose traditions have been shaped by long nights gathered round the flickering flames, whisky and the embroidered tale go naturally hand in hand.

None more so than Highland Park 25 Year Old whose deep golden draught will awaken the fire and the poetry in you

George Mackay Brown was a poet I had quite recently discovered. His work is intricately bound with the people of Orkney, their history and culture. In fact, he saw it as an artistic imperative to re-awaken Orkney to its rich cultural roots, of croft and boat and darkly luminous tales, at a time when he saw these threatened by the plasticity of the technological age and the crass obliteration of progress. Another shade of this is globalisation, loss of identity; and inherent in this for Brown was a culture's loss of creativity. I loved his language, pared down, pristine, accurate: plain and potent as ancient chalk bones. It was exciting to use even a snippet of the poet's words in commercial copy. This was the golden whisky one of his characters might pour from a stone jar on a sunlit afternoon in Hamnavoe. I didn't feel, in any way, that I was debasing Brown's words. Others might disagree. Anyhow, I was to call on his verbal jewel box again but as yet I hadn't even visited this fabled string of islands in the north that is so distinct from mainland Scotland. Highland Park was a good brand to cut my teeth on for many reasons, but particularly because it wasn't burdened with the entourage of traditional Scottish imagery. This was due both to the regionalism of malts mentioned above and to the Norse provenance of Orkney. But quite aside from any of that, what great material for a revenant copywriter now a Johnny-come-lately design writer, an after-hours poet, a secret questor for the truth of myth and language. Whisky had presented me with a bridge between two worlds.

Here was something I could help sell yet remain true, return to and feel energised.

It was around about this time that I learnt about John Simmons[5] through an article in *Creative Review* and sent away to Interbrand in London for a copy of *Telling Stories* (later incorporated into the seminal *We, Me, Them & It: The Power of Words in Business*). John was soon to become the voice for a thousand and more business writers invisible in their solus anonymity and sick to the back teeth with the stale currency of corporate puff and the misguided notion of not only managing directors but also marketing directors that creativity was the visual stuff. Whisky was different. Whisky traded as much with words as with images. I was already telling stories in the commercial world but John articulated the fundamental importance of doing this not just in terms of creative satisfaction but also in terms of making concrete business sense. It's as with people: apart from the infatuations of love and lust, what people look like is not nearly as important as what they say, or indeed how they say it.

Black Bottle, another Highland Distillers brand – this time a blend – gave me my next opportunity to tell a story and turn a phrase. Black Bottle was going through a little transformation. Traditionally, it was a blend associated with Aberdeen in the north east of Scotland that had some Islay malts in it to give its distinctive smoke and pungency. Another such blend is White Horse: its gusto comes from Lagavulin. Anyway, the decision had been made to turn Black Bottle into *the* Islay blend and put some malt from each of the island's seven distilleries into it.[6] All blends these days have "spiritual homes" – one distillery or another – and as Highland Distillers at that time owned Bunnahabhain, Bunnahabhain was Black Bottle's spiritual home.

THE Houla Houla

fling caution to the wind

You won't find this recipe in many books. Which is a shame. It's so simple and just lends itself to primitive spontaneity. For when the dancing breaks out of the fox-trot and becomes a little more 'south-sea island' - undulating and shakin' all over!

2 msr Gloag's Gin
1 msr Florida orange juice
1 dash Curaçao

Shake like the maracas and strain into a cocktail glass over shavings of ice.

10

THE HOULA HOULA FROM THE CAPTAIN'S CLASSIC COCKTAILS – GLOAG'S GIN.

The brand manager was Tim Patterson, with whom I'd already worked on Gloag's Gin. We'd had a lot of fun with that brand. I'd invented a character called the captain who was a wiz at making cocktails and served as the voice of the brand: 40s retro and very lounge lizard Noel Coward. This was a minor brand but if we'd gone to TV I'd always thought that Donald Sinden would be ideal. Tim was on his way up the corporate ladder. And Black Bottle was the next rung. I was teamed up again with Iain Lauder, and Tim wanted us to get a real feel for this island, known as the Queen of the Hebrides. So, we took the 45-minute flight from Glasgow in May 1997. Tim had hired a car and we spent a mad two days taking in various historic landmarks, from Celtic crosses to monuments commemorating sailors drowned at sea. We saw stretches of white sand to die for and seals basking on the rocks at Port Wemyss. We saw Finlaggan, the ancient seat of the Lords of the Isles. We heard tell of dolphins somersaulting in Lochindaal off Port Charlotte – though I was not to witness this until six years later. We were welcomed at Bunnahabhain by distillery manager Hamish Proctor and taken through a tasting session of all the seven Islay malts. And that night we slept in a bed and breakfast on a windswept promontory and joked about what might be in the freezer and the mittened landlady carrying a sharpened axe.

The strapline I came up with for Black Bottle – "Finest Scotch Whisky with a Heart of Islay" – may not have been earth-shattering but I fell in love with Islay. I took my wife and children there later that summer and we've been going back almost every year since. The lyrics of the Islay song that encourage the returning voyager to "say goodbye to care" are not fanciful. Going by ferry is best. The vessels of the downbeat operator Caledonian MacBrayne, which are serving the community over and above the tourist, set the tone. There's nothing pretentious here. This is an island of peat and water and pastureland; it can lash down as if in payment for sin, or shine as if it were a corner of heaven beyond the grid. You relax. The world of time is over the sound. It's open to interpretation, of course. Some sour-faces would say piss and glare. But, indisputably, the whisky's elemental and enjoys wild devotees.

Through writing about whisky I was beginning to discover new regions of this diverse country. The subtle differences not only between one distillery and another, but also between one age expression and another, were beginning in my mind to reflect the subtleties of the landscape over the seasons' cycle. My next trip was to Speyside. Not to work on a Speyside brand, although we were to visit the beat of The Macallan, "the Rolls Royce of Scotch Malt Whisky" (epithetical Jackson again), but at the invitation of Sarah Gilchrist to celebrate the launch of Highland Park 18 and 25 Year Olds. Islay, Orkney, Speyside – all outposts of the Highland Distillers empire (what a long way the industry had come from hiding out in the hills with a pot still). Speyside, of course, is the heartland of whisky, accounting for over half of Scotland's working distilleries. It's a rich, fertile

THE RE-INVENTION OF A BLEND, BESTOWED WITH THE PROVENANCE OF ISLAY,

plain, bordered by mountains through which run the eponymous Spey and its many tributaries like the Livet and the Fiddich. It was golden that autumn and the prospect of fishing on this river famous for its salmon was intriguing. I'd never tried my hand at it before, and we were going to be in the company of the brand's advertising creative from London, Neil Patterson, a Scot and an expert fly fisher.

But before the fishing, the feasting. We stayed at the Rothes Hotel: dark wood panelling, stags' heads, roaring log fires, bulbous plumbing and generous porcelain basins, in fact all the comforts

141

of the Victorian gentry away from their mills and shipyards. This was the best kind of Scottish hospitality, genteel but not stuffy, expensive but also egalitarian. I chucked my hold-all on the bed, opened the throat of the squealing tap to allow a torrent of boiling water to swiftly provide a deep bath and felt immediately at my ease. This was a culture of pleasure, indeed. But rugged not effete, the pleasure of the hunter on scarp and moor to whom silence and wind and birdsong pertain, as well as gunshot and buckling prey. I was the interloper: the chameleon once more, enjoying the ride. But I glimpsed for a moment the ancient heart of this baronial playground, antlered, masculine: noble but deadly. I put on a clean shirt, felt the soft touch of civilisation and went down to dinner concealing, even amidst the trophies, my vision of brown eyes, lead and blood.

What I remember most about that night was not the smoked salmon or the venison by the open fire, or the wines glinting in the crystal glass like liquid jewels or, indeed, the digestifs of Orkney drams in the drawing room, but the connections between the three men gathered together in Speyside to crack open a few bottles of expensive malts and wish them well on their way to market. Unbeknownst to Neil Patterson, after the first gin and tonic, Iain and I were about to spring on him that he knew both our fathers-in-law and my elder brother. Poor Sarah Gilchrist; she had to listen to several hours of exclamations, ramblings down memory lanes and evocations of advertising legends she didn't know a toodley-pip about.

Heroes in an industry of anonymous creators tend to be little known outside its bourn although Sarah would I'm sure have known my father-in-law Vincent Taylor by his campaigns, Direct Line and Intelligent Finance (just unveiling at the time). But Neil knew him from the days of Hall Advertising.

Hall's, as it is generally referred to, no longer exists, but once upon a time it was the creative beacon of Scottish advertising and on a par with London's best. Vincent was the man that made it happen. He took over a provincial bucket shop and transformed it into a star agency. In its firmament were creatives Jim Downie, Neil Patterson and Tony Cox and account man Jim Faulds. After many moons of midnight oil, cold beer and golden gongs, Patterson and Cox headed south, Neil to become creative director of Young & Rubicam and Tony (Iain's father-in-law) to become creative director of DDB then BMP then DDB BMP or some such combination/sequence of self-effacing letters. Jim Downie, with a gang of other Hall's bright sparks, left to set up the Leith Agency. And Jim Faulds set up Faulds. For almost 20 years, Leith and Faulds were the twin pillars of Scottish advertising. Faulds has gone (but not before having nurtured Redpath). Leith lives on but now it too has spawned its own award-scooping enfants terribles. Neil knew my brother Alistair from Young & Rubicam, where he worked as an account director for 20 years. So there we were, truly interconnected. What would E. M. Forster have said?

We were buzzing, even before we cracked into the Highland Park. "Such connections, you understand, haven't helped me a jot in my career," I said to Sarah. In fact, by the time we were on the Cranakin I was more interested in the fact that Iain's wife had once babysat for Jerry Garcia's kids. And it meant nothing to her! I would have baby sat for Jerry Garcia's kids in exchange for an acoustic rendition of 'China Cat Sunflower' any day. Or even 'Sugaree'. But I'm showing my vintage and my proclivities: a motley chameleon. What's all this got to do with Scotch? Only that Scotch has got everything to do with hospitality and conversation. It's at the heart of Scottish hospitality, whether in hunting lodge or town flat. It's become the byword for hospitality the world over from Shanghai to Athens to San Francisco.

I saw my vision of gun smoke in the heather in perspective, as a flashback (with reverberation still). The world of Scotch Whisky is a far wider world now, and that's what I was doing, there in Speyside, trying to extend its reach by forging new imagery and new stories. All this kept bouncing off the inside plating of my skull as I stood in the Spey the next day clad in waders and trying to get that ease of motion that Neil had with his fishing rod.[7] I caught nothing.

* * *

Soon after the trip to Speyside, I left Redpath and joined Scotland's newest advertising agency at the time – The Union. I'd been head hunted. Flattering, but a foolish move for me. I felt too long in the tooth to be writing silly commercials for double glazing and tyre fitting. If you're going to do advertising it's got to be the cream. I left after four months. No shakes to The Union; it grew by leaps and bounds. But I didn't care. The door was still open for me at Redpath and I returned, tail still high, to a cracker of a project with an old favourite Highland Park – and now the reins were in the hands of Tim Patterson (gin › blend › malt).

Highland Park was bottling a 40-year-old whisky from 1958. It was old and rare – just over 600 bottles were taken from cask – and very expensive: £1,000 a bottle. (We now enter the collectors' world of American magnates, Italian dukes and Surrey businessmen.[8]) They wanted to 'add some value', dress up the offering with some choice keepsake accessories. A decanter made of Caithness Glass and engraved with a motif of standing stones was already at prototype stage. And then there was an idea of doing a master distiller's log book, checking the casks through the years. Quite a nice idea but I thought, hang on, here was an opportunity to really weave together the story of Highland Park with the story of Orkney. Forty years is a landmark age for men and women. Benjamin Franklin wrote in 1741, "At twenty years of age the will reigns; at thirty, the wit; and at forty, the judgement." I had just passed my 40th birthday. "The Orkney imagination," wrote George Mackay Brown, "is haunted by time": time stretching way back. And how had these islands and this distillery on the fringes of Europe changed over these 40 years, 1958–1998? How had the making of whisky changed? I wanted to write about all of this. And I wanted to write it in the first person – more like a travelogue than a piece of marketing literature. Which meant a trip to Orkney. It was a tall order (especially as I wanted to take my wife and children). My colleagues at Redpath weren't sure: particularly about the first person approach. But Tim, bless him, said yes.

So, I went to Orkney. And fell in love with Orkney too. My colleague John Ormston thinks I can't resist an island. He's right. I spent three days there with my family meeting and talking with retired distillery workers, getting a feel for the old days at Highland Park. The distillery also organised for a local bus driver, Jim Raeburn, to be our guide around the mainland. They couldn't have chosen anyone better. Jim was a natural storyteller and brought everything alive for us as we hopped from Neolithic remains to the relics of World War II (the grave of The Royal Oak, the boom ships, the Churchill Barriers and one of the most moving places I've ever been, The Italian Chapel). From the stories I gathered, I wrote a short book called *Hourglass: Reflections on Orkney, Time and Highland Park.* It won a Cream Award for best copywriting in 2002. But most importantly for me, it showed me what was possible within the confines of "commercial writing". Here's a chapter about another guy I really enjoyed meeting – Bob Moodie, the still man. Years later, when I saw *Lost in Translation* I thought of Bob and wondered what *he'd* have made of lovely Scarlet Johansson. He shared the same disdain for call girls as Bill Murray's character.

HOURGLASS

REFLECTIONS ON ORKNEY, TIME AND HIGHLAND PARK

By a Highland Park Devotee

CHAPTER THREE

ZEN AND THE ART OF
DRINKING WHISKY

 WAS SITTING IN THE VISITOR CENTRE AT HIGHLAND PARK WAITING FOR BOB MOODIE. He was late, but it had given me the chance to watch the audio-visual programme with the unmistakable voice of Fulton Mackay on the soundtrack. The programme was in the process of being replaced and a film crew had recently been up to Orkney to catch the one week of sunny weather 1998 could muster. Constant liaison with the meteorological office had helped ensure a successful schedule and some glorious sunsets had been captured on camera, a vital requirement to complement Highland Park's bottle label, based on the midnight sun.

Of course, visitor centres, audio-visual programmes and brand merchandise are all modern phenomena, particularly so in the case of whisky distilleries. Looking around Highland Park's tasteful centre, lined with black and gold tubes of 12, 18 and 25 year old malts, crystal glassware

11

HOURGLASS

and stylish gifts, it's hard to think that until relatively recently its consumption as a single malt was limited to discerning Scots and a modest number of international cognoscenti. Today the cat is well and truly out of the bag and malt whisky is one of Scotland's most inspiring and sought-after exports.

Times have changed, but a tour of the distillery and talking to the men who worked there, shows that the essential process of distillation remains the charming mix of inherited craft and inexact science it ever was. Reassuring for the connoisseur, as the wonder of malt whisky is that each is unique, an inimitable expression of the place from which it hails, its geological and climactic conditions, and the methods and instruments of production employed there.

What have changed are, in many ways, trappings and inessentials, though not any the less interesting for that. Computerisation and mechanisation have played their inevitable part in streamlining old ways and minimising certain tasks. Peter Swanney remembers filling in exactly the same forms year after year. Things were constant and familiar. George Guthrie remembers there being up to thirty or forty men out on the moors cutting peat in the summer. It's more like a handful today.

In the old days, any one of the distillery workers would break off from the job in hand to show visitors around. Peter Swanney remembers taking visitors up onto the kiln floors to see the greenish columns of heavy, peaty smoke rising

12

ZEN AND THE ART OF DRINKING WHISKY

through the wire plates to malt the barley. Although this is not allowed today due to Health and Safety regulations, one of the joys of visiting Highland Park is seeing smoke billowing from the twin pagodas that loom over the distillery. Today, most distilleries' pagodas are cold and merely decorative as their barley is malted elsewhere, but Highland Park, along with only a few others, continues to do its own malting. First the barley is laid out to germinate in the 'barns', then re-laid for drying and flavouring on the floors above the great kilns. The sweet honey smell of crackling heather and the sight of the fibrous brown clods of peat ablaze beyond the cast-iron kiln doors remains for me a vibrant, organic image at the heart of Highland Park's creation.

It would have been very much at the heart of the distillery in 1958 too. A black and white photograph of Highland Park in 1958 that hangs in the visitor centre shows the oriental-looking lumbs smoking away. What it also shows is the distillery, and its outlying barrage of warehouses, surrounded by acres of fields and well outwith the boundaries of Kirkwall. The population increase in Kirkwall, referred to earlier, was obviously partially accommodated in these neighbouring fields. In the 1960s and 1970s new housing estates gradually closed the gap between distillery and capital, and now Highland Park is a bastion of tradition on the edges of lamp-lit avenues and groves. Estimating the value of the vast number of casks (45,000 or so) quietly at rest in the string of warehouses across the

13

road from the distillery it also struck me that this place was somewhat akin to Fort Knox. Particularly as Highland Park's deep, amber malt is known to many as 'Orkney's Gold'.

As I was musing along such lines Bob Moodie showed up. With a shock of white hair, neat beard, steel-rim glasses and lumberjack shirt he certainly looked the part of home-spun stillman. But any preconceived notions as to the type of man that he might be were quickly dispelled. Bob's reason for being late was that he'd been looking after his grandson, an assignment that included feeding and changing. Crooning too, I thought as I tuned in to Bob's melodic voice.

Lynne Linklater, the visitor centre manager, ensconced us with a dram of the splendid 18 year old (there wasn't a trickle of the 1958 in sight, being kept for altogether more rarefied customers) and Bob filled me in on his background. The Moodies had farmed on Stronsay for generations, though Bob's father had himself worked at the distillery – in the fifties there had been three or four 'sets' of father and son at Highland Park. Bob had initially learnt the skills required to be a millwright, at a time when each parish had its own mill for grinding bere[1] to make Orkney bannocks – round flat cakes. But wisely, as the mills subsequently went into decline, Bob turned his hand to joinery. As it turned out, shift-work at the still house meant that over the years

[1] I have since learnt that bere – a rare genus of barley – has been found to be identical to that grown in ancient Egypt. If this is true, it shouldn't be too surprising as Orkney was a trading post thousands of years ago.

14

ZEN AND THE ART OF DRINKING WHISKY

a multitude of small joinery jobs around the house piled up that he promised his wife he'd sort out when he retired. Three months after Bob left Highland Park his wife died. He still felt guilty he said, taking a sip of his whisky and looking sombrely into the middle-distance.

"What has been the biggest change at the distillery since 1958?" I asked Bob. "The Health and Safety Act," he replied. Before this came into force the opportunity had been there for workers to help themselves to a dram here and there throughout their shift. Sometimes this was a communal partaking, as in the 'rolling dram' that Peter Swanney told me about. When the filling was completed, casks were rolled into the warehouse and the call of 'rolling' went out so that every available worker could come and lend a hand. This done, everyone passed the Brewer's office and received a dram, gathering together to have a chat and a smoke with their whisky. However, as Bob explained, self-discipline was required – especially amongst workers whose jobs required accuracy and judgement, as did his in the still house – for the 'whisky' drammed was clear pre-cask spirit and very penetrating indeed. Reading between the lines, Bob applauded the Act as it did the workers a favour and a more sensible regime operates today whereby workers get an altogether smoother dram after their shift and half price bottles in perpetuity, when they retire.

Though an appreciative but perspicacious drinker (he spoke scathingly of drunkenness) Bob had an extraordinary

15

story to tell of how he became the archetypal Scotch drinker. Two Japanese businessmen visited Highland Park "in them days when I had a fine head of hair and my beard was much wilder, not trimmed as it is now" said Bob. They spotted him about the yard and started to talk animatedly. Bob thought nothing of it, but not long after he received an invitation from a Japanese advertising agency to go to Osaka to act as a model for a poster and television campaign. All he had to do was be himself, and sip whisky.

Bob wasn't sure whether to go, but his wife said it was the opportunity of a lifetime. So he went. He spent ten days in Osaka, staying with a local family at night, and every day just being himself, sipping whisky, looking the archetypal Scot (or rather, Orcadian, which as we now know is slightly different) and worrying whether they could understand his accent. On his last night he was taken out for a lavish celebration meal by the agency, and after much sake and Scotch Whisky and Japanese whisky (which Bob generously described as "lovely") one of the account executives said to him: "I envy you, Mr. Moodie, going where you're going later tonight." Bob gazed at him steadily and, irrespective of local protocol, took the cue to make his excuses, saying, to the affrontery of the Osakan adman, that he was ready for his bed. Far from home, in exotic surroundings, feted and having had more to drink than usual, Bob remained true to himself. A good man to drink with. He seemed to endorse what Neil Gunn wrote in his thought-provoking classic 'Whisky

16

ZEN AND THE ART OF DRINKING WHISKY

and Scotland' – "distillery workers as a class of men are amongst the most trustworthy and obliging and pleasantly mannered . . . " As he drove me the mile or two back into Kirkwall Bob told me that he'd recently struck up a relationship with a widow from his home island, Stronsay. Twenty years his junior, the widow had thought she'd never get involved again, but, she'd told Bob, she felt relaxed with him. I felt genuinely pleased for him. Perhaps he'd have time now to put up shelves and make cupboards.

17

1. Now no longer true as Blackwood distillery has set up in Shetland.

2. Whisky brand bibles are usually rather hefty tomes, either expensively bound or manual-like in a daunting lever-arch file. They are usually a mix of brand guidelines (colour pantones, fonts, use of photography etc.) and stories and anecdotes about the brand to convey its flavour. So, they're a lot more interesting than brand guidelines in other sectors. My partner and I have done The Macallan, Glengoyne, The Glenrothes and Glenmorangie as well as Highland Park but I was particularly pleased with the playing card idea. Unconscious inspiration, I'm sure, came from Jamie Byng's inspired re-issue of the Bible in separate pocket-sized books (the Canongate pocket canons) with introductions from the likes of Doris Lessing, Blake Morrison and Will Self. They're now getting great writers like Margaret Atwood and Jeanette Winterson to re-tell the Greek myths. Brilliant.

3. All you have to do to become a "friend" of Laphroaig is to buy a bottle of 10 or 15 Year Old and send in the barcode. It's fun. The whole brand espouses the craik around drinking whisky and uses language to great effect. Ardbeg, down the road from Laphroaig, is a great brand and a great dram too. They don't need to take themselves too seriously. This year, they ran a poster campaign around the revolution theme with distillery workers dressed up as Che Guevara and Castro. I love the photograph on page 183. It encapsulates so much about the best of Scottish humour – eccentric and down to earth. This combination, as well as a penchant for smoky iodine, obviously appeals to Prince Charles as well. Laphroaig bears the coat of arms of the Prince of Wales. A perfect offset to the gloomy Port Ellen bar.

4. The Glenrothes – up until now pretty much a connoisseur's brand but used as the heart of Cutty Sark – has pursued the vintage concept, which works very much along the lines of wine vintages. Limited quantities of the very best casks of Glenrothes malt whisky are individually selected, from a given year's distillation, when judged to be at the peak of their perfection and bottled as The Glenrothes Vintage Malt. Those casks that are selected must meet the malt master's exceptionally high standards. In addition they must have other characteristics so special they warrant bottling as a "vintage". Not all the casks from one year will meet these strict criteria and a vintage is not guaranteed each year. Seeing as The Glenrothes is 50 per cent owned by Berry Brothers & Rudd, the famous London vintners it's unsurprising maybe that they've applied the viticultural approach to whisky. Another great brand. And I'm hoping that if I say enough nice things about them they'll invite me to Rothes House which, as I myself have written "originally belonged to the Church and

maintains an atmosphere of repose, study and quiet retreat" and I'll enjoy an informal ceremonial dinner in the beautifully furnished "barn". A version of Scottish hospitality written about but not tasted. The life of a copywriter is sometimes damned hard. I could re-write the myth of Tantalus for Canongate.

5. I had actually heard of John Simmons some years before when I was working with John Mitchinson, the marketing director of Waterstone's, to launch a new offering, Waterstone's Reading Holidays. John Simmons was helping to prepare the first brochure at Newell & Sorrell. John Mitchinson left Waterstone's before the holidays were launched, the new regime axed the project and my wife and I subsequently set up our own operation, Bloom Reading Holidays. That's another story. Even so, all stories are connected. "It was a wild and stormy night. We put a bottle of malt on the table. Our stories criss-crossed the globe."

6. Islay's seven distilleries that contribute to Black Bottle: Ardbeg, Bowmore, Bunnahabhain, Bruichladdich, Caol Ila, Laphroaig and Lagavulin.

7. Flyfishing was, and I'm sure still is, Neil's passion.

8. Probably the world's most expensive bottle of whisky was sold in May 2005. A businessman paid over £32,000 for a bottle of Dalmore 62 Single Highland Malt Scotch Whisky, at the Pennyhill Park Hotel, Bagshot, Surrey. Only 12 of the bottles were produced in 1942. The hotel reports that the man bought the bottle and drank most of it in one night with five incredibly lucky friends. The identity of the buyer remains a mystery, but he is a regular hotel guest and a collector of spirits. The man kept the bottle and the presentation case as a memento. Each of the bottles has its own hand-printed label and unique name. This one was called the Matheson, named after the owner of the Dalmore Estate. One bottle has been kept by the brand's owner Whyte & Mackay and the other ten are in private collections. The Matheson may be the first bottle opened and enjoyed by its owner. We can only wonder who or what the mystery man was celebrating or mourning.

CHAPTER 9
2020
NEW WORLD

In the cabin by the Pacific Emilia, you will remember, has fallen asleep. Lachlan has deftly undressed her and laid her on the bed, naked except for the map he'd found in her bag. The map Emilia had folded up and brought from John Damian's. His words, charting the journey of barleycorn to whisky. What he thought as he spread the map from her mass of hair (now threaded with silver) to her wild lowland grasses (still black as charcoal) was how, as recently as the turn of the century, whisky had not been sexy. But how that had changed. How the sensual had won through, and Neil Gunn's "penetrative" spirit had been feminised. The brand had found its anima. Retraced its steps to its origins in the perfumeries of Arabia. Its tastes of fire and sea and honey evoking a new language. There was, of course, world enough for tobacco reek and gun oil and even, sadly, the blood and glass of bar-room brawls. But this enduring spirit, which had overcome punitive taxes, the unwanted attention of the excise men and prohibition,1 which had grasped opportunity when it had presented itself, with the demise of brandy and the rise of the Empire and the vast Scottish diaspora, itself created as much out of adversity as enterprise, this enduring spirit had, in the kindling years of the new millennium, overcome the crisis of identity in its own backyard and risen like a phoenix or a Venus de Milo. He gazed at the tablecloth map, creased at the folds but essentially flat atop the contours of her body. The map breathed as she breathed.

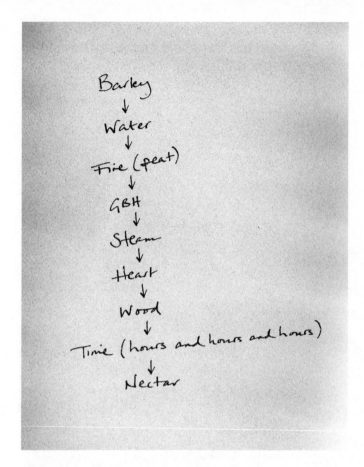

Then he took his notebook and wrote:

Barley her hair, water her tears, fire the red of her mouth. GBH: he winced and kissed the hollow between her collar bones. Heart her heart, hidden but always manifest, wood the cask of her womb. Time, the hours of joy in loving her, nectar the taste of her, in flower and chant and ecstasy.

Then he turned the map so that the process started where life starts and ended at the crown, where pleasure is bliss, the sensual is spiritual.

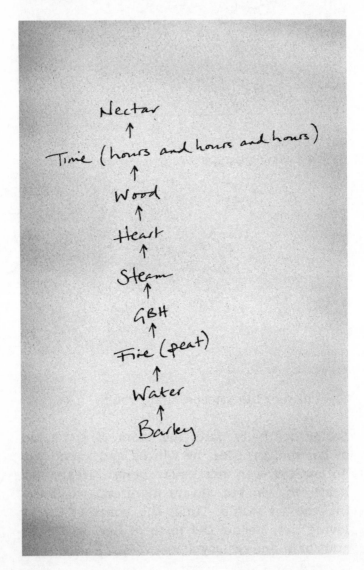

And he wrote:

I think of Burns now: 'Coming Through The Rye' and 'Green Grow the Rashes O'. Songs that are straightforwardly erotic in their evocation of sexual attraction and consummation. The waters break, the child is born. The fire of the emotions leads to hurt and bruising until it transforms into something pure. Then it settles in the heart: anger becomes justice, joy compassion. But to mature, the spirit must enter the wood, the dark of unknowing, the voyage through the starlit ocean of illusion, the sea of infinite inter-reactions. It will take hours, days, years. Everything that's good grows. Over time, we come to love. We think we love our children straightaway. But they've been coming all our lives – to remind us who we are and where we're going. Coming to break our hearts, coming through the rye.

Well that's a variation on John Barleycorn, Lachlan thought as he gently lifted the map off Emilia's body. Death and resurrection in the twenty-first century. Whisky, the spirit of contemplation. And consolation. He pulled the sheet and quilt up under Emilia's chin and kissed her forehead.

...AND IT IS STILL LIGHT AND THE SUMMER NIGHT
LENGTH AHEAD PEELING THE TISSUE FROM THE
NEW CHIFFON LEMON FROTH FROCK AND HONEY
GLOVES SLIPPING TOGETHER AND HONEY HEELS
LIKE CHAMPAGNE GLASS STALKS SUCH EXTRA
VAGANCE! TO BED ANCED TO RUIN ON A NIGHTS
WORTH OF FLOOR A NIGHTS WORTH OF NOSTALGIA
OH FOR THE FILMS WE COULD STAR IN IF WE WERE
BEAUTIFUL HIM AT THE DOOR IN THE GRAND SUIT
WITH TIE IN HAND DANGLING AND A BOTTLE TO
NOW START THE SPELL AND THE KITCHEN SPILLING
DISHES FROM THE HURRIED TEA WASHING ON THE
PULLEY A WHITE CLUTTER OF SHIRTS AND SOCKS
AND UNDER THINGS AT OUR EARS LIKE CLUMSY
CATKINS HE SAYS YOU RE A DAFFODIL TONIGHT
AND ZIPS ME TIGHT Y ELLOW UP THE BACK TILL I'M
STIFF AS HE IN THE DARK POSH SUIT AND UP RIGHT
LIKE A DANCER AND WE'RE TWO PEOPLE MIGHT
SUDDENLY TAKE A TAXI ANYWHERE O ANYWHERE
BUT ALWAYS TO A BALL THE RADIO PLAYS AN OLD
ACCORDION AN OLD MAN'S TUNE FOR TAPPING
TO WE HOLD EACH **N°7** OTHERS' STRANGE
SHOULDERS IN THE KITCHEN AND SWAY

N°7
SINGLE CASK
SCOTCH MALT WHISKY

I BENEATH THE SOCKS
HAND STANGLED AS IF THEY WERE EACH OTHERS'
FASTER BIRLING FASTER TILL WE NEARLY TAKE OFF
INTO THE LAUNDRY **BOTTLED BY** AND FLY INTO THE
FAR **THE SCOTCH MALT WHISKY SOCIETY** SKY
AND AFTERWARDS THE BREATH BIRLED RIGHT
OUT OF ME HE KISSES ME A TONGUEFUL OF WHISKY
THAT CHASES INTO MY THROAT AND TRAVELS
BELLYWARDS **CASK NO. 41.33** AND OUT TO MY
SKIN ENDS **AGED IN OAK 14 YEARS** WHERE IT
SITS LIKE A PERFUME O! MY BREASTS ALL WHISKY
AND THEN HA ASKS ME WOULD YOU TO SAY AYE
MY WEE DAFT DAFFODIL AND
50cle AYE IS AYE AYE I WILL AYE. **60.4%vol.**

PRODUCED IN SCOTLAND

AFTER CHANEL – JULES HORNE AND NINA GRONBLOM'S STRIKING LABEL FOR 26 MALTS

1. **Prohibition** In Prohibition, there was for Scotch Whisky once again, in the wake of adversity, opportunity. In particular, the Scottish whisky distillers responded energetically, if clandestinely, to US Prohibition, which lasted 13 years between 1920 and 1933. In cahoots with backers from the City of London and freelance ships' captains, whisky was shipped in bulk to the Caribbean islands and then sold on the black market to American racketeers. One of the most famous "rum runners", as they were called, was Captain McCoy, from whom we get the phrase "The Real McCoy", indicating that the quality of whisky was assured. The demand was there, and brands like Cutty Sark took a foothold and, after the ban was lifted, strode in to dominate the US drinks market, now the biggest single Scotch Whisky market in the world.

CHAPTER 10
§2
DE'IL'S
ADVOCATE

Just as the angels were congratulating Azrael on his sterling work, who should show up on the crest of Stac Pollaidh but the Fallen One. Brighter but not bigger than her old class mates, Lucifer liked to appear as a woman, a normal sized woman. She was not particularly beautiful. But she was sexy and strangely comforting. A lot of people fell for her. She knew just how bad you were, and she didn't care. In fact she was wont to say, "You could be worse darling. You could be a lot worse than that!"

She'd come to claim whisky as her own. After all, she had all the best tunes. Why shouldn't she have the best booze as well? What she loved best of all, of course, was to cause a bit of a stir. These angels and their eulogising of whisky! Nectar and other such pap! The stuff was the ruin of many a good man and woman. As she well knew. It was her ally. It was damnation in a bottle and had the lick of hell fire. And best of all she had some of the most famous of Scottish writers to argue her case.

Like Napoleon, she had a travelling trunk of books. She liked Scots writers. They did a good line in dark. The chill factor, of course, can put you more in touch with your skull and bones than other, more temperate climes. But traditionally there has been, in Scots folklore and literature, a fascination with demonic possession or as poet Iain Crichton Smith used to say "murder and graveyards". That's why Shakespeare got away with his Macbeth, because the character was true even if not factual.

An Iago-like imp was carrying the trunk strapped to his reddish back. He unbuckled it and set it down at his side. He turned to her, and showing his long yellow teeth in an ingratiating smile, he offered to get her favourite references lined up. "I'll be my own advocate, thank you, "she said, freezing the smile on the demon's face to a miniature Fingal's Cave.

The angels were edgy. They knew what was coming: the "hard man" image of Scotch and the withering literary endorsements; the other side of the Victorian coin, the bad, adulterated whisky and the ruin and rot equal to gin. You couldn't deny it. Whisky, like the world itself, had a chequered history and the devil would hop from dun to charcoal check. She'd cite Stevenson, of course, and claim that the potion Dr Jekyll blended that turned him into his other self, Mr Hyde, was none other than a brew of whisky. She'd cite the twentieth century writers who pulled no punches when it came to denouncing the hard stuff as a key contributor to a protagonist's decline, starting with the seminal Scottish novel of the twentieth century *The House with the Green Shutters* written by George Douglas Brown in 1901, in which a son kills his tyrannical father stoked with the courage or "smeddum" of blended whisky. In Lewis Grassic Gibbon's *Sunset Song* of 1932 a thoughtful, pacifistic young man is driven by taunts of "coward" to enlist in the army and do his bit in the First World War. He returns to his wife unrecognisable. Brutalised by army experience, he's now a hard drinker. She saves herself from a wife-battering only by defending herself with a kitchen knife. The spiritual fall of a Scot is indicated by an escalating reliance on the hard stuff.[1] Lucifer would here deride the regimental imagery used by brand creators of the elegant, upright officer and the noble kilted soldier with his busby and pipes. "Hard to square," she'd say, "with the stories of brutal initiation rites, fuelled by drink, that surface in the papers every so often!"

She'd zip to the latter end of that "century of the novel". "The last bastion of truth!" she'd cry tauntingly, echoing maybe the greatest claim for the novel form, gleeful at the chance to use truth for her own designs. She'd cite Johnnie Stark the "Razor King" from *No Mean City* and the work of William McIlvanney and James Kelman, and relish the narrator's summary of Glasgow (Scotland's touchstone) in Alasdair Gray's 1982, *Janine*: "Glasgow now means nothing to the rest of Britain but unemployment, drunkenness and out-of-date radical militancy." Then, riding high in her metaphorical saddle of triumph – and this is what the angels hoped for – she'd make her fatal flaw by straying into the higher reaches of literature, poetry. She'd cite what is arguably the defining Scots poem of the twentieth century, Hugh MacDiarmid's 'A Drunk Man Looks at the Thistle'. "Says it all," she'd say.

"Ah Lucifer," Raphael would reply, Raphael being the scholar, "blinded by your own brightness. You've always debated whether it was you or God who was in the detail. The lawyers would have it that it's you. But when did they ever inspire anyone? When it comes to verse, the alchemy of language, you should slow down. The Drunk Man makes an onslaught on the hard stuff that passes as whisky in Scotland. He's making a distinction between malts and blends. Which explains the lines from Norman MacCaig's 'Ballade of Good Whisky' of 1962 addressed to the older poet: 'Here is a toast you won't scunner at/Glenfiddich, Bruichladdich and Glengrant!' And when Burns wrote 'Whisky and Freedom gang the gither' there was, of course, only malt."

* * *

Let's leave the angels, fallen and uplifted, arguing it out on the ridges of Coigach. It's an old chestnut. Neil Gunn argues a similar case to Raphael's in his *Whisky and Scotland* of 1935. It's a highly romanticised depiction of malt whisky as the magical distillation of the Celtic people, the gentle sweet-talking Gaels. It's as much a caricature as the macho Scot blootered on the national sauce – even if I did pinch my title from it! Read it. It's stirring stuff.

The fact is, as I said earlier, whisky's a tiger whether you're talking malts or blends. Or, to get the element right, a shark. It's the water of life, after all. Water can be gentle and lull you to sleep or dash you to your death on the rocks. In 1977, I went to hear the Tibetan Lama, Chime Rinpoche speak in Oxford. He was explaining the take of the different schools of Buddhism on the illusory nature of life – a key tenet of eastern philosophy. His parable centred on a poison berry, whether it was real or not and what one should do about it. The Hinayana Buddhists, said Chime, say the berry isn't real – turn your back on it. The Mahayana Buddhists, he continued, say the berry is an illusion – so ignore it. The Vajrayana Buddhists, his own school of the Diamond Way, say: it's real, it's poisonous, it's no illusion, eat it. Somewhat nearer to home but echoing the Lama's words are Sir Robert Hamilton Bruce Lockhart's in his 1959 *Scotch*, where he says: "As an enemy there is no Scot who does not know its dangers, and almost no Scottish family without its whisky skeletons. They rattle in my own cupboard and I myself have been near enough to destruction to respect whisky, to fear it and to continue to drink it."

Drunkenness and violence, of course, are often the result from feeling powerless and oppressed, factors that have marked large swathes of not only Scottish society but also societies everywhere. As far as I can see there are two answers: 1) empower people; and 2) take personal responsibility. The industry today – and all the brands within it – advocates responsible drinking. The cynic might laugh and say "moderation hardly ties in with increasing volume sales". A baker wants to sell all the loaves she bakes each day but she hardly wants anyone to go home and gorge themselves on her dough and get colic! Whisky is a product that must

PRODUCT OF SCOTLAND

COMPASS BOX

CRAFTED WHISKIES

Hedonism

An extraordinarily rich and sweet whisky.
Not chill filtered. Natural colour.

Vatted Grain
Scotch Whisky

43%vol   COMPASS BOX WHISKY, 24 GREAT KING ST. EDINBURGH, SCOTLAND   70cl e

live or die within a competitive market. It can increase sales against competitor spirits. It's doing that. It can also genuinely advocate responsible drinking. My knowledge of people within the industry who are not just making the stuff but selling it is that they're decent folks not evil purveyors of the primrose path. Most of them, probably – and some of them definitely – get pissed sometimes. I think the industry's got it just about right and I like what John Glaser founder of Compass Box (handcrafted small batch Scotch whiskies in distinctive and original styles) says about the big buzz – corporate social responsibility – on his website:

> I believe that people need to feel deeply and passionately about what they do – about the products they create and sell. I believe that a business has an obligation to contribute to society by supporting the welfare of its community. I believe this obligation should be integrated into a company's work. It should be part of the belief system of all the people who join the company ... I believe that running a business in this day and age comes with certain obligations. Here are some of my thoughts.

Business is the most powerful force in society today. Ben Cohen and Jerry Greenfield of Ben and Jerry's ice cream fame write an insightful piece on this topic in their book *Ben & Jerry's Double Dip*. Their thoughts have reinforced my views on the subject, and I thank them for that. They point out that in past centuries religion was the most powerful force in society, and with that status came the role and obligation of churches to promote the general welfare of society. Over time, this power and its associated obligations shifted to governments. But today, business has taken over as the most powerful force in society.

And with this role should come (I contend) the same obligation as churches and governments have had in the past: the obligation, as the most powerful societal force, to support the community and promote its general welfare. Community can be defined differently by different businesses, but I believe that at minimum it refers to the employees of the company, and the community where the company operates or where its business activity has the greatest impact.

So what can I do about this obligation as a tiny start-up company? From a strictly local perspective, I can support local suppliers for everything from office supplies to the printing of my whisky labels. From a broader perspective, I can do things that support sustainable environmental business practices, like sourcing paper for my labels and stationery that is made of unbleached fibres (versus paper from bleached fibres, whose production can pollute water sources with toxins). And this is harder than it sounds, because these alternatives are often more costly, which is sometimes a difficult choice for a small business to make. I therefore believe it's even more incumbent on bigger businesses to try to make these decisions to help bring down overall costs of these alternatives.

From a long-term perspective, I hope that the sales of Compass Box whiskies, which draw on whiskies from distilleries all over Scotland, will support the livelihood of these distilleries and the jobs associated with them; many distilleries in Scotland (particularly those in remote regions with little else in the way of industry) are susceptible to closure through industry consolidation and rationalisation. If Compass Box can play a part in helping generate greater demand for whisky in the world, these distilleries and their jobs are more secure.

Another thing we can do is to set aside a percentage of before-tax profit every year to give back to the community in some form of support. As we're a small business, it's not a great deal of money, but it's something. An important something, I think.

There has to be some irony here from the *Double Dip!* Words of wisdom from the ice cream parlour! Mitres give way to cones, cassocks to aprons, censers to ladles. But yes, it's true. It has to be a good path to follow.

The Compass Box brand hits other spots for me too, mainly in the totally fresh approach to the brand imagery. There's a feminisation, a balancing, a tempering of the masculine and, behold, there's an alchemical feel to the brand. Look at the images – what do you think? They're a hit in the style bars of London, a precursor maybe to San Francisco's John Damian's. Such feminisation, I contend, is a crucial step the industry needs to make. I have played a small part, with the 26 Malts project with the Scotch Malt Whisky Society.[2] If you think by feminisation I mean pink ribbons and girlie stuff please stop reading. I mean the integration of the anima with the animus. I believe the sensory approach to whisky is the key – a drink to be savoured not swilled.

Today, all Scotch Whisky brands advocate responsible drinking,[3] and major brands are high profile on the sponsorship front, giving back to the community in a significant way. Famous Grouse is the sponsor of Scottish Rugby Union. Glenfiddich sponsors "The Spirit of Scotland" award every year, which celebrates outstanding Scots in all walks of life. Glenfiddich also sponsors six artists in residence to work in galleries every year at the distillery in partnership with Arts and Business Scotland. Bowmore sponsors the Blair Atholl showjumping event every year and The Macallan joined forces with *Scotland on Sunday* to set up the most prestigious and well paid short story competition in the UK (it's now passed on to Orange and *The Scotsman*). And according to Daigeo's website, Diageo has committed one per cent of its operating profit to social investment and community projects – currently an input value of over £17m annually. Part of this investment is made by the Diageo Foundation, set up by the company to offer "kick-start" funding and expertise for projects within priority themes.

More "behind the scenes" is The Robertson Trust, established in 1961 by the Miss Robertson Sisters. Miss Elspeth, Miss Agnes and Miss Ethel Robertson inherited, from their father William, a controlling interest in Robertson & Baxter and Clyde Bonding Company now known as The Edrington Group. The 1961 Trust Deed transferred, into a charitable trust, most of their shareholding in the two companies. The Trust Deed had two main objectives: the first was to ensure that the company remained independent; the second was to ensure that dividend income from the shares would be given to charitable purposes. The Misses Robertson were trustees for a combined total of 71 years, which ensured that the trust was established using the guidelines that they had used for their family business. The Robertson Trust currently disburses £6m a year.[4]

These are just a few examples of the industry giving back to the community. And just the other day, listening to the pure strains of Barnsley folksinger Kate Rusby in Edinburgh's Usher Hall,

I thought what a long tradition there was of a proportion of the profits of whisky being ploughed back into society. One hundred and fifty years later we can still hear, in concert, the echoes of Andrew Usher's millions. What's still to come – and this I'd dearly love to see – is an industry-wide initiative tackling a global problem like water shortage in the world's poorer countries. What if the "water of life" got behind Water for Life and donated £1 for every bottle of Scotch Whisky sold towards finding a solution for those who have no water?

ANDREW USHER

I'd like Scotch Whisky to rise to such a height. Then, of course, its esteem in the world would become unparalleled. Lucifer would be appalled. And we could re-phrase Holinshed thus: "It windeth up the old crusties, it spitteth out the feint hearted, it weedeth out the low brow whiners, it speaketh volumes for the nation's creativity, it reeketh of unbridled joy and ingenuity, it challengeth the status quo. It cutteth to the quick the detractors. It lighteth up the welcoming lamps of reason and

setteth them on high branches in the forests of cant and confusion. It masheth the spuds of the fur-hatted competitors and hast them beeling. And in the words of the saint that evoketh the almighty who setteth all worlds to right – all shalt be well and all shalt be well and all manner of thing shalt be well when the shit hitteth the fan and the spirit and her materials are one".

1. Read Alan Bold's insightful essay in *Scots on Scotch* edited by Phillip Hills, Mainstream Publishing.

2. 26 Malts was a collaboration between The Scotch Malt Whisky Society and 26, the national organisation that champions the more creative use of language in business communications. Twenty six writers were teamed up with 26 designers, and then taken through a Scotch Malt Whisky Society "three malts" tasting, at which the colourful language of aroma and taste as used by the society was explained. The idea of the task ahead was not to emulate this language but to respond to an unidentified whisky as artists not experts, and to use the senses as guides to a creative response, the form of which was to be a unique label.

   Each team was duly given an unidentified sample of cask-strength malt whisky. The malts evoked some amusing and powerful responses, all of which are recorded in the book *26 Malts: Some Joy Ride* published by Cyan.

   The results included poems, fibs, teasers, salutations, invitations, trompe l'oeils, talking whiskies, responses inspired by tarot and alchemy, bananas and liquorice, rubber tyres and the sweetest of golden honeys. Twenty-six labels liberated from usual brand constraints – all testifying to the provocative complexity and allure of Scotch Malt Whisky.

3. The Scotch Whisky Association is strong on this and has a natty strapline – "Matured to be drunk responsibly".

4. From the Robertson Trust's website, *www.therobertsontrust.org.uk*

CHAPTER 11
2006
A SHORT FINISH

It is a dark and stormy night ... rain pelts the roof slates, branches whip the window panes ... the logs in the grate are diaphanous, incandescent ... crack open a bottle of whisky...tell me a story. Wherever you are in the world, when the whisky hits your senses, return here – to Scotland. It is a dark and stormy night ... rain pelts, branches whip, logs glow, whisky flows. Tell me a story. You wanted something concrete? Why? After all, this is a spirit. The Scots are known the world over as being great rationalists, pragmatists, but, as Bruce Lockhart said, "Whisky has saved us – otherwise we would be so infuriatingly efficient."

I've told you a story. I've tried to capture something about Scotch the brand past present and future. I'm interested in the future. I work in the field of marketing. We in marketing always seek to breathe and taste the future. I'd love to see John Damian's for real. I'd love Highland Park to create a brand called Preacher's Silence. Many whisky brands have the potential to create universal mythologies rooted in their particular location and unique stories. Everything's possible. The legendary Ardbeg is back in production cleverly titillating its loyal followers with early-age bottlings in preparation for the return of the 10 Year Old in 2008. We already have wood finishes (not juniper yet – but we'll see). We already have brave new pioneers like The Easy Drinking Whisky Company with their iconoclastic approach to blending and their cut-the-crap fun marketing. We already have Rachel Barrie's stylish 60 per cent Nichol Baillie Jarvie, William Grant's Monkey

LOOKING FOR AN 18 YEAR OLD AT THE ISLAY FESTIVAL – POSTERS OF ARDBEG REVOLUTIONARIES ON THE WALL

Shoulder triple malt (named after the temporary injury suffered sometimes by malt men in turning the barley by hand) and J&B's pale whisky –60C , as white as a white spirit. And we already have Compass Box with Peat Monster, Hedonism and Eleuthera. Now, too, we have the Scotch Malt Whisky Society's 26 Malts and although stocks are limited and unrepeatable the experiment in "freeing the spirit" will hopefully bear fruit. But that's another story, another book.

What can we learn from Scotch the brand? The long-running strapline of The Famous Grouse says it all really: "Quality in an age of change." You could transpose the word consistency for quality. The key to this is alluded to in another long-running famous strapline – Glenmorangie's – "Hand crafted by the sixteen men of Tain." A consistent product, skilfully made, from one country – Scotland – and, in the case of malt, from

183

Whisky
Without The Waffle

The True Story
of
Jon, Mark & Robbo's
Easy Drinking Malt Whisky

www.jonmarkandrobbo.com

one place and one place only, like Tain. The product is the bedrock of the Scotch brand. But, as we've seen, the story of Scotch is also one of opportunism, nerve and flair. A forerunner in the worlds of advertising, packaging and brand imagery, Scotch has a bright future. After all, it's golden. Here are ten lessons from Scotch the brand. But I who propose them would probably be more gainfully employed going to Bruichladdich's Whisky School on Islay and learning a little more about this intriguing spirit.

1. Have a great product
2. Modernise but never at the expense of traditional craft and skills
3. Ensure that your people are passionate
4. Realise the value of protective laws
5. Be prepared to innovate within strict parameters – in fact, the stricter the parameters the more creative the challenge
6. Use your provenance, but respond to changing perceptions of that provenance
7. Variations on a theme mean there is room for countless interpretations in terms of brand imagery
8. Use the senses: they're the door to the heart and the imagination
9. Be bold. Be top of your world. Be around tomorrow. And tomorrow. And, for good measure, tomorrow.
10. Where myths are made about kings and nations, brands have everything to play for.

Tell me a story. If it's good, I'll buy your poison. And if that's good I'll come back for more.

ACKNOWLEDGMENTS

This book was born out of firsthand experience, research and talking to people. So, many to acknowledge: the first being my dad for creating an early association in my mind between 6pm and amber; the second my mum, for being his smiling partner in crime; the third my wife, for allowing the poison in the house but mostly for being my enduring rock and shining light of reason.

Then, beyond the family, I have to thank John Simmons, without whom this book would never have happened – thanks for the faith and the opportunity. And then, long-time design partner Damian Mullan, without whom this book wouldn't look half as good as it does. Illustrator Kim McGillivray for his special treatment of the cover. Publishers Cyan – Martin Liu for staying steady after the shock of reading draft 1 and Pom Somkabcharti for never giving up. Fellow Dark Angel, Jamie Jauncey, who encouraged me to take the imaginative route with this story.

And fellow 'tooth' John Ormston for his constant support and wry humour.

And the people I've met and learnt something from in the various worlds of whisky:

Glenmorangie's Master Distiller Bill Lumsden for his insights into the secrets of wood. And for Glenmorangie's Master Blender, Rachel Barrie for helping me see into the olfactory world with her deft use of language.

Hamish Torrie for blowing the mothballs out of the Ardbeg legend with a huge sense of fun.

Easy Drinking David Robertson ('Robbo') for giving up the Rolls Royce for a surf board.

Compass Box John Glaser for waving goodbye to the big boys and heading in his own, unique, direction.

Charles MacLean (Mr Whisky) for his time, his encyclopaedic knowledge of whisky and his encouragement. And for graciously being seen to take a potato tasting every inch as seriously as a whisky tasting one very daft night in the old village hall.

David Williamson of the Scotch Whisky Association for his fine overview of the industry and permission to reproduce some of the Association's hard facts and figures.

A succession of Highland Park brand managers: Sarah Gilchrist, Tim Patterson and Nicole Walton; each one of them a fantastic client, dedicated to the brand but genuinely open to creativity.

Special thanks to Tim for believing in my maverick approach whilst others (sans suits) who should have risked more, sat on the fence. Designer Iain Lauder for sharing the Highland Park years and revelling in the nonsense of purple prose.

Charlotte Halliday of the Scotch Malt Whisky Society for saying 'yes' to 26 Malts: a brave yes. Her colleague, Annabel Meikle, for bringing whisky tasting alive with panache and feminine charm.

Iain Crichton Smith, one of the funniest people I've met, for revealing so much of the Highland psyche. My neighbour Black Aonghas Macneacail, crowned Gaelic Bard of Scotland, who not only provided the wee translation at the front of this book but who also introduced me to Talisker, the malt of his native Skye.

Also for sharing this wonderful exchange between two coves brought up under the severity of the Wee Frees: "It's not that we shouldn't enjoy ourselves Murdo: we shouldn't enjoy enjoying ourselves."

Hamish Proctor, former distillery manager of Bunnahabhain, for taking me through the seven malts of Islay. Ian Macpherson (AKA Percy), distillery manager of Bowmore for popping open the wood matured range when I was stuck on the island. Andy Hibbert, who was with me, for suggesting we hire a helicopter to get me off; for later bearding two Brummies in the Harbour Inn and almost convincing them that our film for the distillery was heading for the Oscars. We ended up doing something completely different. And used actor David Rintoul for the voice over. Talking over the air between London and Glasgow studios

David told us this story of Islay hospitality. After a day's sailing off the coast of the island he and his party rowed in for a drink in Port Ellen. As he approached the dim-lit no-frills bar a man turned on his stool and without a flicker or a beat spat: "You're the cunt that plays Finlay." As they say in Gaelic, céud míle fáilte – Scotland extends 'a hundred thousand welcomes'. These little gems are at two ends of the spectrum.

DIGGING PEAT. LONG MAY IT CONTINUE.

BIBLIOGRAPHY

Allen Andrews, *The Whisky Barons*
(The Angels' Share, 2002)

H. Charles Craig, *The Scotch Whisky Industry Record*
(Index Publishing Limited, 1994)

Stuart Delves, Jamie Jauncey and Damian Mullan (eds),
26 Malts: Some Joy Ride (Cyan Books, 2005)

Tom Devine, *The Scottish Nation: 1700–2000*
(Allen Lane, 2000)

Hugh Douglas, *Bonnie Prince Charlie in Love*
(Alan Sutton Publishing Ltd, 1995)

John Glaser, the Compass Box website 2005

Neil M. Gunn, *Whisky and Scotland*
(Routledge, 1935)

Phillip Hills (ed), *Scots on Scotch*
(Mainstream Publishing, 1991)

Michael Jackson, *Malt Whisky Companion*
(Dorling Kindersley, 2003)

Charles MacLean, *Scotch Whisky: A Liquid History*
(Cassell Illustrated, 2003)

Charles MacLean, *Scotch Whisky*
(Mitchell Beazley Pocket Guide, 2002)

Alistair MacLeod, *No Great Mischief*
(Jonathan Cape, 2000)

John Simmons, *We, Me, Them & It*
(Cyan/Marshall Cavendish, 2006)

PICTURE CREDITS

Pictures on pages 11, 88, 89 and 92 courtesy of John Dewar & Sons.
Thanks to archivist Jacqui Seargeant

Picture on page 12 courtesy of Charlie MacLean's collection

Picture on page 15 courtesy of Chris Miller and Susanna Freedman

Pictures on pages 19, 24, 44, 60, 64, 86, 101, 103 courtesy of Glenmorangie
plc. Thanks to B. A. Nimmo

Pictures on pages 20, 23, 54, 59, 83, 90, 91, 178 and 189 courtesy of Diageo. Thanks to archivist Christine McCafferty

Picture on page 27 courtesy of Sara Sheridan and David Freer

Picture on page 33 courtesy of Kate Patrick and Ron Burnett

Pictures on pages 36 and 173 courtesy of the Compass Box, London. Thanks to John Glaser

Picture on page 41 courtesy of Whyte & Mackay. Thanks to Richard Paterson

Picture on pages 51, 161 and 162 courtesy of Lachlan McAllister

Picture on page 67 courtesy of Henzteeth – design by Damian Mullan, illustration by Kim McGillivray

Picture on pages 78/79 courtesy of Chivas Brothers (Pernod Ricard)

Picture on page 81 courtesy of William Grant & Sons. Thanks to Chris Rigby

Picture on page 97 courtesy of John Allert and Patrick Bergel

Picture on page 108 and 113 courtesy of The Walter Scott Digital Archive, Edinburgh University. Thanks to Paul Barnaby

Picture on pages 120 & 121 courtesy of The Trustees of the National Library of Scotland. Thanks to Jenny Parkerson

Picture on page 123 courtesy of Matthew Fitt and Damian Mullan

Pictures on pages 131, 135, 138 and 148–155 courtesy of The Edrington Group. Thanks to Jason Craig

Picture on page 141 courtesy of Burn Stewart

Picture on page 164 courtesy of Jules Horne and Nina Gronblom

Picture on page 179 courtesy of 26

Picture on page 183 courtesy of Ardbeg. Thanks to Hamish Torrie

Picture on page 184, courtesy of JMR Easy Drinking Whisky Company. Thanks to David Robertson

On page 40 I wanted to illustrate the text with the vignette from *The Crab with the Golden Claws*. However the constraints on reproduction laid out by the Hergé Foundation and Moulinsart SA include: 'It is not allowed to reproduce visuals from the work of Hergé in a financial, political, medical or paramedical framework or in a context related to weapons and alcohol.' (Note the *and* not *or*.) A shame, especially as since I wrote the book I've learnt that 2007 is Hergé's centenary. Would someone write a play called *Tintin in Purgatory* in which our hero meets up with all the baddies from all the adventures plus a few real ones from our own times, our own shores even. And Captain Haddock can keep the whole thing jolly and counterpointedly briny with a case of Laphroaig. He'll have graduated to malts.

OTHER GREAT BRANDS STORIES

ADIDAS *All Day I Dream About Sport: The story of the adidas brand* by Conrad Brunner

ARSENAL *Winning Together: The story of the Arsenal brand* by John Simmons & Matt Simmons

BANYAN TREE *A Brand Born of Romance* by Andy Milligan

BECKHAM *The Story of How Brand Beckham was Built* by Andy Milligan

DYSON *The Domestic Engineer: How Dyson changed the meaning of cleaning* by Iain Carruthers

eBAY *The Story of a Brand that Taught Millions of People to Trust One Another* by Elen Lewis

GOOGLE *Search Me: The surprising success of Google* by Neil Taylor

GUINNESS *Guinness is Guinness: The colourful story of a black and white brand* by Mark Griffiths

HARRY POTTER *Wizard!: Harry Potter's brand magic* by Stephen Brown

IKEA *A Brand for All the People* by Elen Lewis

INNOCENT *Building a Brand from Nothing but Fruit* by John Simmons

STARBUCKS *My Sister's a Barista: How they made Starbucks a home away from home* by John Simmons

UNITED STATES *Brand America: The mother of all brands* by Simon Anholt & Jeremy Hildreth